Dr. Luke Discusses Discipleship

sharing "your" gospel story

(A Devotional Study Guide of the **Book of Acts**)

Written, Revised and Compiled by:

Dr. Garry Baldwin

© **2018** by Dr. Garry Baldwin

Scripture references: Holy Bible, Holman Christian Standard, Pew, Maroon (Holman Bible Pub) © 2012

What has Jesus done in your life story? Is He a part of it? The world is waiting to hear about Jesus. The world wants to discuss the authenticity of the faith message from your life. The world is not interested in just a historical story though, but it is looking for a transforming story. How does the historical Jesus still change lives today? And how has Jesus gotten involved in your life story? Do you need some examples of sharing your personal gospel story? This is the purpose of this Bible Study through Acts. It is a discussion about discipleship. It is a discussion about how to learn and apply the faith message in a significant and authentic way in your life. It models as is discusses discipleship (how to share your gospel story).

The book is known as The Acts of the Apostles. It is "praxis" in Greek which means "great deeds of the apostles or "significant believers." This is correct, though it mostly tells us of the acts of two apostles. Acts begins with Peter, (Acts 1-12), whose ministry was to the Jews and whose great word was 'repent' ; and ends with Paul, (Acts. 13-28), whose ministry was to the Gentiles and whose great word was 'believe'. However, this book does not record the acts of men but of the Risen Lord, who by the Holy Spirit filled and used men as His instruments. It is a authentic discussion of significant discipleship. In Acts 1:1 Luke tells us that in his Gospel he recorded " all that Jesus began to do and to teach..." For 33 years the Holy Spirit had indwelt, filled and worked through the human body of the Man Christ Jesus; then this same Man returned to heaven and the Holy Spirit came and filled His mystical body, the Church, and so the Lord continued to do His mighty works from heaven. Dr. Roy Taylor (my mentor) said "a better title for this book is 'The Acts of the Holy Spirit'". And... because of this the Book of Acts is an unfinished book; it records the continuing work of the

Holy Spirit in His Church. It includes "your story" as a part of 'His' story. Luke wrote his Gospel and also the Book of Acts (compare Luke 1:1-4 and Acts 1:1)- Both letters were written to Theophilus. As the only Gentile writer (Colossians 4:10-14) in the New Testament in his 2 books (Luke and Acts) we find 27.5% of all the writings of the New Testament. He was a disciple and a disciple maker.

Written about AD 63 and covering approximately 33 years of history Acts is a biography of the beginning of the Church. Interesting that our Lord Jesus was on the earth for 33 years, and in Acts we have an example of what can be accomplished through one generation of believers (33 years).   Acts 1:8 is the key verse of Acts:

"But you will receive power when the Holy Spirit has come upon you, and you will be My witnesses in Jerusalem, in all Judea and Samaria, and to the ends of the earth."

Thus the book divides naturally according to this key verse. The first seven chapters record the Lord Jesus Christ at work by the Holy Spirit through the apostles in Jerusalem. Here the church is established. Chapters 8 through 12 record the Lord Jesus Christ at work by the Holy Spirit through the apostles in Judea and Samaria. Here the church is enlarged. The remainder of the book (chapters 13-28) is devoted to the Lord Jesus Christ at work by the Holy Spirit through the apostles unto the uttermost part of the earth. Here we see the church expanded.

It is a fact that every Church dies and replaces itself on a continuing basis. As the Church gets "older" (in membership ages) it will either replace itself by revitalization with new younger members or die from within. Statistics show that about 5000 plus Churches will close their doors this year. When I read that statistic from *Lifeway,* I had to think, what can a Church do to avoid being a statistic? This is a major "storm warning" indeed.

This book will help you learn to do something.

How? What if every older more mature member of God's Church began to invite, disciple, and train someone to take their place when they go to heaven? What if our generation discipled and trained *"Generation Next"?* What if we took this storm warning seriously? The Church would grow and continue as we follow God's Word in 2 Timothy 2:1-2 which reads: *"You, therefore, my child, be strong in the grace that is in Christ Jesus. And what you have heard from me in the presence of many witnesses, commit to faithful men who will be able to teach others also."*   This has been my heartbeat at in ministry for many years, but now as the faithful die and age out we must intensify the effort. The future of the Church is upon us and the Vision to "make disciples" and "be witnesses" must be passed on to the next Generation of believers to carry the torch of God's Word and to stand firm in the faith. As we walk through the book of Acts and discuss discipleship with the author of Acts, "Dr. Luke" it will be transferred as a lifestyle as we apply these principles together "heart to heart". It is time to "Be Alert" and "Act". God is wanting to use His Church in your Church and community to reach *"Generation Next".*

Why are we using the book of Acts? Well several reasons come to mind. It is authentic (2 Timothy 3:16); it is the first book ever written of church history; it is the history book of the Church, of which we are members; and it applies to this Church age and the dispensation of the Holy Spirit in which we are living . It is full of discipleship instructions that can be applied as you reach out to

"Generation Next". It is our textbook (2 Timothy 2:15); that we teach us how to worship, walk, witness, and win souls. It tells us how the early Christians gave, worked together and acted in times of crisis! What an exciting record it is! **It is a clear doctrinal study.** In Acts we hear the gospel preached and see it working. We hear it in the sermons and speeches of Peter, Paul, Stephen, Philip, James and Ananias, and quickly learn what a Christian believes and how he is to present the gospel to others. All the vital doctrines are emphasized in this book, and it is significant to notice that the message, though preached by many different people, is always the same. The Book of Acts seems to be the authentic missionary manual of the Church, dealing with the why, the how and the where of missionary work. "It speaks of the evangelization of cities (Acts 8:1-8), of individuals (Acts 8:26-39); and it shows how men are called and equipped for missionary service."

But as J. Vernon McGee summarizes: "The Book of Acts is not complete. It breaks off with Paul in his own hired house in Rome. It has no proper ending. Do you know why? It is because the Book of Acts is a continuing story. Perhaps the Lord has Dr. Luke up there writing the next chapters now. Perhaps he is recording what you and I do for Christ in the power of the Holy Spirit. I hope so."

I want to thank the staff and lay leaders of Brookwood Baptist Church, in Burlington, N.C., who, over 20 years ago in 1996, helped put the original format of this study guide together along with many great thoughts as I compiled their insights and inspirations. Together, we learned to grow in the faith and live our lives by God's Grace in that faith journey. Together we began this project. I want to thank my secretary and discipleship encourager Mona Hearne, who has served beside me for over 30 years, who still disciples others and models this book. She spent many hours typesetting and reviewing this project. I want to thank my son Caleb who is always an encourager and a servant as he designed the cover of this project. I want to thank my son Jeremiah who provided some "English tutoring" and suggestions in the linguistics of this project. And finally I want to thank my co-laborers in Ministry at Midwood, my wife of 42 years Cheryl, and my daughter Anna Grace who help promote, support, and serve wherever they are asked to. I love you all, Thanks!

This guide is to help the reader to walk through the book of Acts and apply it to their faith walk today in order to live out their faith daily as they ask the LORD for directions and help. Begin in silence as you seek the presence of your Heavenly Father and God. Continue in confession as He convicts and cleanses your heart. Then, listen for a fresh Word from our LORD who will speak to you at your personal point of need.   In such a time as this in our world, one has to know where they stand on issues that demand an example of that lifestyle. My prayer is that this study will allow you to join with me in sharing our gospel stories with relevance and authenticity.

My Daily Quiet Time Journal
(How to use your Acts devotional guide)
As you begin your Daily Quiet Time follow the guide located on the right side of the page. Use this space to journal your thoughts and prayers. Refer to this guide for details of how to journal your journey.

1. **Ready** yourself for a ***Fresh Encounter*** (Seek and recognize God's presence as you begin your time.) *"Be silent before the LORD and wait expectantly for Him."* Psalm 37:7 Do this in Prayer using this ACTS guide:

a.   **A**doration: (Praise and Worship) Psalm 100:4
"Enter His gates with thanksgiving and His courts with praise: give thanks to Him and praise His name."

b.   **C**onfession: (Repentance and Forgiveness)
"...forgive us our sins, as we ourselves also forgive everyone in debt to us." Luke 11:4

c.   **T**hanksgiving and **S**upplication (Praise and Asking)
"Hallelujah! Give thanks to the LORD, for He is good: His faithful love endures forever." Psalm 106:1

2. **Read** God's Word.

Read today's Scripture and hear a ***Fresh Word*** from God. *"All scripture is inspired by God (God-breathed) and is profitable for teaching, for rebuking, for correcting, and for training in righteousness."* 2 Timothy 3:16

Then... as you journal...Write down your thoughts about what you are hearing God say in the space provided and

3.   **Respond** with the ***"Mind of Christ."***
This is your hearts response to God's Word. This may include questions where fuller understanding is needed as well as petitions for personal needs, and intercession for others.   (Write them down in the space provided)
"I assure you, anything you ask the Father in My name, He will give you." John 16:23

Then...*Continue to write down your reflections...*

4. **Reflect** and listen to God's voice. (This is God's response to your prayers.) What is God saying to you? How has He answered your prayers? Record these truths *"Call on me and I will answer you and tell you great and unsearchable things you do not know."* Jeremiah 33:3 Then...

5. **Rely** on Jesus to help you live out these truths.
   (My response to what God has told me to do.)
"Those who hear the Word of God and keep it are blessed."
Luke 11:28
Ask the Lord, "What do you want me to do today?"

These are your most important parts of your journaling...Listen to God's Voice and record what you hear

a. God's to-do list for today.
(List things you feel you need to do.)

b. Put on the full Armor of God:
"Stand firm then, with the belt of truth buckled around your waist, with the breastplate of righteousness in place, and with your feet fitted with the readiness that comes from the gospel of peace. In addition to all this take up the shield of faith, with which you can extinguish all the flaming arrows of the evil one. Take the helmet of salvation and the sword of the Spirit which is the Word of God." Ephesians 6:14-18

"And pray in the Spirit on all occasions with all kinds of prayers and requests." **Pray continually.**

Remember that this guide is for you to journal your journey and write down what you are hearing God say to you as you are in prayerful conversation with your God and Master. He is speaking to your heart. Hear Him and Obey Immediately!

Week One - Day One
Acts 1:1-5

Great Things Ahead

Having completed his first book, (The Book of Luke) Luke continued to write. He wanted to make sure that there was a clear understanding of God's Word. He wanted to assure his people that God's Word was for all people and that it was for all churches. The Book of Acts reveals much about the worth of an individual and how God, through the power of the Holy Spirit, can use the church to overcome persecution, prejudice, politics, pride, greed, geography, and other hindrances. This Book completes God's instructions to the disciples and provides a coordinated account of the beginnings of the Church, and your calling.

In verse four, Luke invites us to listen to one of the intimate, quiet conversations between the risen Lord and His closest followers. This conversation provides the motivation for another principle of discipleship: purity of life. Jesus clearly gives His command, "Do not leave Jerusalem, but *wait* for your gift" . . . the greatest gift which the Father promised, "baptism of the Holy Spirit". Do you think the Apostles had a problem with waiting? They had been with Jesus for three years and He was a doer/teacher. His witness was straightforward and positive. Jesus was a man of action and the Apostles were accustomed to going, doing, praying, preaching, and working. Now Jesus instructed them to wait. Wait for the promise of the Father. Today it is the "prompting" of the Spirit we are waiting for. It is our directions for the day.

In our "instant" society, waiting can be the hardest thing required of us. But we must wait. The best is yet to come!

My Quiet Time Journal

1.   **Ready yourself** for a Fresh encounter with God.   Pray and ask God to speak to you. (Psalm 37:7)

2.   **Read** the Scripture of the Day and prepare to hear a **Fresh Word** from God. (II Timothy 3:16-17)

3.   **Respond** with the *"Mind of Christ"* by writing down what God has said to you through the Scripture and the devotional thoughts. (Jeremiah 33:3)

4.   **Reflect** as you *"Experience God"* by listening to His Voice and writing down your prayers and thoughts.   (John 16:23)

5.   **Rely** on Jesus to help you live out these truths. (Luke 11:28) Ask, *"Lord, what do you want me to do today?"* (God's to-do list.)

(Pray for strength as you put on the Full Armor of God.)

Acts: 1:6-11

He Will Come Back

As a believer in Jesus as our Lord and Messiah, we are expecting that He will come again. Are you ready? Or do you wait and then start getting ready later, taking a chance that Jesus will wait around for you to decide if you want eternal life, to decide if you want to receive power and be His witness? Tomorrow could be too late, not only for you, but for those to whom Jesus commanded you to witness to. Are you ready disciple? Are you ready to help others grow? Jesus' last command to the Apostles was for them to witness to the ends of the earth. They were to turn their attention to the most important activity in life: bearing the name of Jesus to those next door and then to those in the uttermost parts of the world. They were to be like pebbles dropped into a pond which would generate ripples in ever-widening circles even unto the ends of the earth. This is still our calling. This is still our command to follow. "He appointed twelve - designating them Apostles - that they might be with Him and that He might send them out to preach." (Mark 3:14) He still is appointing disciples. We must disciple "Generation Next".

Our response to the "come unto Me" of Jesus (Matt: 11:28) should also become the responsibility to obey the "go" of Jesus. (Matthew 28:19) We are saved to serve. We do not witness because we are redeemed to witness, we are called to witness and when we do Jesus goes with us!

So the URGENT task is the message that comes through to us as we listen to the Lord Jesus describe His strategy for world evangelism. There is no time to lose. The command of Christ is clear: "You will be My witnesses." (Acts 1:8)

My Quiet Time Journal

1. **Ready yourself** for a Fresh encounter with God. Pray and ask God to speak to you. (Psalm 37:7)

2. **Read** the Scripture of the Day and prepare to hear a **Fresh Word** from God. (II Timothy 3:16-17)

3. **Respond** with the *"Mind of Christ"* by writing down what God has said to you through the Scripture and the devotional thoughts. (Jeremiah 33:3)

4. **Reflect** as you *"Experience God"* by listening to His Voice and writing down your prayers and thoughts. (John 16:23)

5. **Rely** on Jesus to help you live out these truths. (Luke 11:28) Ask, ***"Lord, what do you want me to do today?"*** (God's to-do list.)

(Pray for strength as you put on the Full Armor of God.)

They All Joined Together

Christ's followers, numbering about 120, gathered in the upper room. "They all joined together *constantly to pray*." (Acts l:14) Peter called their attention to the Scriptures which spoke of a replacement for Judas. Peter said, "It is written in the book of Psalms,

'May his place be deserted; let there be no one to dwell in it, 'and, 'May another take his place of leadership.'"
(Acts 1:20)

They prayed and searched the Scriptures. What were they looking for and what were they praying for? These followers knew that Jesus did not leave any unfinished business. They knew He would show them His will. Jesus would pick the person to lead them. It was their responsibility to search and pray constantly until they received an answer. God had a plan for His people. He still does.

What about you? What do you do when it's your responsibility to select a leader? Do you make sure that you recommend one of Christ's followers? Do they love Jesus with all their heart? Or do you look for a popular, successful business person or someone with many credentials? Jesus didn't think any of the above reasons were important. As a matter of fact, all the persons that you see in the Scriptures were ordinary people. But it was their intimate, personal relationship with God that made them extraordinary. We are called to train and develop the next level of leadership in the Church. God wants us to disciple the next generation of leaders.

How is your relationship with our Lord? Are you ready?

My Quiet Time Journal

1.   Ready yourself for a Fresh encounter with God. Pray and ask God to speak to you. (Psalm 37:7)

2.   Read the Scripture of the Day and prepare to hear a **Fresh Word** from God. (II Timothy 3:16-17)

3.   Respond with the **"Mind of Christ"** by writing down what God has said to you through the Scripture and the devotional thoughts. (Jeremiah 33:3)

4.   Reflect as you **"Experience God"** by listening to His Voice and writing down your prayers and thoughts. (John 16:23)

5.   Rely on Jesus to help you live out these truths. (Luke 11:28) Ask, **"Lord, what do you want me to do today?"**   (God's to-do list.)

(Pray for strength as you put on the Full Armor of God.)

Acts 1: 21

Choose One

How does God show us His will? Well, Jesus was the very best model. He completed every assignment God gave Him. He never failed to do the will of God. He obeyed.

John 5:17, 19-20 helps us to understand how Jesus came to know and do the will of God. "Jesus said to them, 'My Father is always at His work to this very day, and I, too, am working.'" He wants to lead us and help us lead.

"Jesus gave them this answer: 'I tell you the truth, the Son can do nothing by Himself; He can do only what He sees His Father doing, because whatever the Father does the Son also does. For the Father loves the Son and shows Him all that He does. Yes, to your amazement He will show Him even greater things than these.'" The Apostles also knew this. They searched the Word trying to discern the will of God. Then they acted on what the Lord showed them. They were His men, it was His work, let Him decide. So the Apostles offered two men to watch over the ever-growing flock of God and to co-labor with them in the ministry. God was ready to lead these who submitted to the calling. God is ready to use us also for His Glory and our good. God is wanting to disciple us so we can disciple others who are called. He wants us to trust Him.

ISN'T IT A RELIEF TO KNOW THAT GOD WILL MAKE ALL THE DECISIONS FOR US IF WE ASK HIM?

My Quiet Time Journal

1.   **Ready yourself** for a Fresh encounter with God. Pray and ask God to speak to you. (Psalm 37:7)

2.   **Read** the Scripture of the Day and prepare to hear a **Fresh Word** from God. (II Timothy 3:16-17)

3.   **Respond** with the *"Mind of Christ"* by writing down what God has said to you through the Scripture and the devotional thoughts. (Jeremiah 33:3)

4.   **Reflect** as you *"Experience God"* by listening to His Voice and writing down your prayers and thoughts. (John 16:23)

5.   **Rely** on Jesus to help you live out these truths. (Luke 11:28) Ask, *"Lord, what do you want me to do today?"*   (God's to-do list.)

(Pray for strength as you put on the Full Armor of God.)

The Replacement

The replacement must come from the company of men who stayed together, who witnessed Jesus' baptism by John, who witnessed the Ascension of Jesus and His Resurrection. In other words, the one chosen must be a follower, a witness, and a true and faithful servant of our Lord, Jesus Christ.   Generation Next is around us. We must look for these who will replace us in serving the LORD.

God, through His marvelous wisdom, grace, and love for His people, desires to help His people be their best and do their best. He provides overseers - spiritual leaders - those whose experience in the ministry and years of devotion to Christ can be drawn upon by younger workers in the harvest.   These overseers can visit the younger in the flock, pray with them, and share ideas.   Leaders must be diligent in the attention they give to those they are leading. Proverbs 27:23 says, "Be sure you know the condition of your flocks, give careful attention to your herds."

Acts 20:28 "Guard yourselves and all the flock of which the Holy Spirit has made you overseers. Be shepherds of the church of God, which He bought with His own blood."

BEING A LEADER IS SERIOUS BUSINESS. LEAVING A FLOCK UNATTENDED, UNPROTECTED, UNLOVED, AND UNCARED FOR IS SEEN BY GOD AS GROSS NEGLIGENCE, A SIN OF THE WORST KIND

And So God is calling His people to carry out His plan to go and make disciples of all nations. God is wanting to use you

My Quiet Time Journal

1.   Ready yourself for a Fresh encounter with God. Pray and ask God to speak to you. (Psalm 37:7)

2.   Read the Scripture of the Day and prepare to hear a **Fresh Word** from God. (II Timothy 3:16-17)

3.   Respond with the *"Mind of Christ"* by writing down what God has said to you through the Scripture and the devotional thoughts. (Jeremiah 33:3)

4.   Reflect as you *"Experience God"* by listening to His Voice and writing down your prayers and thoughts. (John 16:23)

5.   Rely on Jesus to help you live out these truths. (Luke 11:28) Ask, *"Lord, what do you want me to do today?"*   (God's to-do list.)

(Pray for strength as you put on the Full Armor of God.)

Acts 1:23-25

They Proposed Two

In verses 24 and 25 it says, "Then they prayed. 'You, oh God, know everyone of us inside and out. Make plain which of these two men You choose to take the place in this ministry and leadership that Judas threw away in order to go his own way." As they continued to seek God's will they were looking for an overseer who had love, patience, and the ability to encourage and inspire those he would lead. They proposed two and either would be great.

When a leader disciples younger workers and comes across as a cold, mechanical, and demanding person, he will naturally meet with resistance from those he wants to help. Leaders must not be overbearing. They should imitate the One who was meek and lowly of heart. His ministry and relationship to those in it should be patterned after the life of the Chief Shepherd. As they met and prayed together they were becoming united in spirit and purpose.

Who tells you whom God wants to serve as a Deacon, a Pastor, or a Teacher? GOD DOES! In the Church does God instruct one person one way and someone else another way? NO! GOD WANTS UNITY AMONG THE BODY!

Paul said in I Corinthians 1:10, "I appeal to you, brothers, in the Name of our Lord Jesus Christ, that all of you agree with one another so that there may be no divisions among you and that you may be perfectly united in mind and thought." God gives us perfect directions as we trust Him.

NOW...THEY WERE READY TO CAST LOTS AND TRUST GOD

My Quiet Time Journal

1. **Ready yourself** for a Fresh encounter with God. Pray and ask God to speak to you. (Psalm 37:7)

2. **Read** the Scripture of the Day and prepare to hear a **Fresh Word** from God. (II Timothy 3:16-17)

3. **Respond** with the *"Mind of Christ"* by writing down what God has said to you through the Scripture and the devotional thoughts. (Jeremiah 33:3)

4. **Reflect** as you *"Experience God"* by listening to His Voice and writing down your prayers and thoughts. (John 16:23)

5. **Rely** on Jesus to help you live out these truths. (Luke 11:28) Ask, *"Lord, what do you want me to do today?"* (God's to-do list.)

(Pray for strength as you put on the Full Armor of God.)

They Trusted God

The first chapter of Acts ends with the eleven Apostles letting the Lord choose the right man to take up the ministry of an overseer. They chose two and then used the Old Testament method of letting the Holy Spirit make the final decision. They cast lots. Generation next was chosen.

Do you think the people in "your church" follow the example of the Apostles and the followers we have learned about in this chapter? Do you gather together and pray before you vote? To know God's will you must pray and ask God what He wants you to do. But first - in order for you to know God's will you must know Him!

I Cor. 2:14 says, "The man without the Spirit does not accept the things that come from the Spirit of God, for they are foolishness to him, and he cannot understand them, because they are spiritually discerned."

As God talked to the disciples about things concerning the kingdom of God, He will talk with you. But you must know Him. It is through an intimate love relationship that God reveals His will to you. You just have to decide if you are going to do what you want to do and ask God to bless it, or if you are going to pray and ask God to show you where He is working, and join Him there!

"It is God who works in you to will
and to act according to His good purpose."
Philippians 2:13

Following Jesus one day at a time will keep you
in the center of God's will!

My Quiet Time Journal

1.   Ready yourself for a Fresh encounter with God. Pray and ask God to speak to you. (Psalm 37:7)

2.   Read the Scripture of the Day and prepare to hear a **Fresh Word** from God. (II Timothy 3:16-17)

3.   Respond with the *"Mind of Christ"* by writing down what God has said to you through the Scripture and the devotional thoughts. (Jeremiah 33:3)

4.   Reflect as you *"Experience God"* by listening to His Voice and writing down your prayers and thoughts. (John 16:23)

5.   Rely on Jesus to help you live out these truths. (Luke 11:28) Ask, *"Lord, what do you want me to do today?"*   (God's to-do list.)

(Pray for strength as you put on the Full Armor of God.)

Acts 2:1-11

The Disciples Multiply

Acts 2 celebrates the birthday of the church. It took place during the feast of Pentecost, a harvest festival, fifty days after the Passover. The curious events that confront us in this passage must be looked upon in the light of the Great Commission of Christ. (Matt. 28:18-20) In fact, everything in life, everything in history, everything in the church must be looked upon in that light. We must govern our lives in light of Christ's Great Commission. That must be a major factor in any decision we make. Trying to satisfy ourselves with earthly activities when we were made for heaven is foolishness. But with Christ at the center of our lives, and His Commission burning in our hearts, life becomes what it was meant to be - filled with adventure, excitement, meaning, and purpose. As Acts 2 reveals, the Apostles made that discovery. As Peter and John reflected on the Great Commission, I'm sure the magnitude of the mission Christ had given them overwhelmed them. How could they share the gospel in a meaningful way with a Parthian, a Mede, an Elamite, or someone from Mesopotamia? They had probably never even met anyone from Mesopotamia, Cappadocia, Egypt, or Libya! But if they worried about that, they were concerned about the wrong thing, because Jesus had it all planned. The Lord Jesus simply gave the Apostles a head start. He brought the Parthians, Cappadocians, Egyptians, and others to them. He also gave the Apostles the ability to communicate the gospel clearly in the foreigner's languages.

Jesus has it all planned. He still does. We just need to follow His lead. "Generation Next" is waiting.

My Quiet Time Journal

1. **Ready yourself** for a Fresh encounter with God. Pray and ask God to speak to you. (Psalm 37:7)

2. **Read** the Scripture of the Day and prepare to hear a **Fresh Word** from God. (II Timothy 3:16-17)

3. **Respond** with the *"Mind of Christ"* by writing down what God has said to you through the Scripture and the devotional thoughts. (Jeremiah 33:3)

4. **Reflect** as you *"Experience God"* by listening to His Voice and writing down your prayers and thoughts. (John 16:23)

5. **Rely** on Jesus to help you live out these truths. (Luke 11:28) Ask, *"Lord, what do you want me to do today?"* (God's to-do list.)

(Pray for strength as you put on the Full Armor of God.)

Acts 2:12-21

The Word in Our Hearts

At this point Peter did an amazing thing. Rather than be offended by this accusation, or get into an argument, he simply quoted a passage of Scripture. Most of us would be hard pressed just to stand up and quote Joel 2:28-32 as Peter did. Remember he hadn't just come from his study with a sheaf of notes in his hands. He was in the street. He had no prepared sermon. He simply stood up and quoted the Bible. Where did he get that idea? The answer is simple. He had walked for three years with One who, when He was accused or challenged, would often say, "Haven't you read in the Law?" or "Have you never read in the Scriptures?" or "Have you not read in the book of Moses?" and then Jesus would quote the Bible. (Matthew 12:5, 21:42, and Mark 12:26) Peter was mightily fortified by the Word of God in his heart. As we reflect on this simple truth, it becomes obvious that our lives and witness would improve if we would engage in the diligent practice of Scripture memory. But there's a problem. Now the devil also has a long memory. He remembers as if it were yesterday the day he and Jesus had it out on the mount of temptation. Three times he tried, and three times Jesus completely devastated him with the Word of God. Satan remembers. When we become motivated to saturate our hearts and lives with the Scriptures, he will do everything in his power and pull every deceitful lie out of his bag of tricks to stop us. He cannot face the Word of God head on and win. And he knows it. Focus on studying and memorizing God's Word and share it with others.

My Quiet Time Journal

1.   Ready yourself for a Fresh encounter with God. Pray and ask God to speak to you. (Psalm 37:7)

2.   Read the Scripture of the Day and prepare to hear a **Fresh Word** from God. (II Timothy 3:16-17)

3.   Respond with the *"Mind of Christ"* by writing down what God has said to you through the Scripture and the devotional thoughts. (Jeremiah 33:3)

4.   Reflect as you *"Experience God"* by listening to His Voice and writing down your prayers and thoughts. (John 16:23)

5.   Rely on Jesus to help you live out these truths. (Luke 11:28) Ask, *"Lord, what do you want me to do today?"*   (God's to-do list.)

(Pray for strength as you put on the Full Armor of God.)

Acts 2:21-28

The Gospel

In Peter's sermon he preached the Gospel, which is the power of God. Paul summarized the Gospel by saying, "For what I received I passed on to you as of first importance: that Christ died for our sins according to the Scriptures, that He was buried, that He was raised on the third day according to the Scriptures, and that He appeared to Peter, and then to the Twelve." (I Corinthians 15:3-5) Christ died - that's history. He died for our sins-- that's good news.

What happened as a result of his preaching? "Those who accepted his message were baptized, and about three thousand were reaped into the kingdom of God on this great harvest festival." (Acts 2:41)

As we observe Peter we exclaim, "What a man! What a great servant of Christ!" Yes, that's true. But to keep things in perspective, look at the last verse of the chapter. The believers were "praising God and enjoying the favor of all the people. And the Lord added to their number daily those who were being saved." (Acts 2:47) It wasn't Peter; it was the Lord who was doing it all. This is the first great principle of witnessing for Christ: God does it. God is the one who brings the harvest. He just wants us to obey His directions. The second principle is that He uses people. When those two great principles gripped my soul, it was such a release. I was no longer under a burden. It was not my work, it was God's! And, praise His name, He wants to use us! If you will grab hold of this truth it will allow you to witness the truth of God and trust Him for the results. God is wanting to change our world through us.

My Quiet Time Journal

1. **Ready yourself** for a Fresh encounter with God. Pray and ask God to speak to you. (Psalm 37:7)

2. **Read** the Scripture of the Day and prepare to hear a **Fresh Word** from God. (II Timothy 3:16-17)

3. **Respond** with the *"Mind of Christ"* by writing down what God has said to you through the Scripture and the devotional thoughts. (Jeremiah 33:3)

4. **Reflect** as you *"Experience God"* by listening to His Voice and writing down your prayers and thoughts. (John 16:23)

5. **Rely** on Jesus to help you live out these truths. (Luke 11:28) Ask, *"Lord, what do you want me to do today?"* (God's to-do list.)

(Pray for strength as you put on the Full Armor of God.)

Acts 2:29-36

Christ and Lord

Jesus came from Heaven to Earth to show the way. From the earth to the cross our sins to pay. From the cross to the grave. From the grave to the sky. And we will exalt His name on high. God has made this Jesus ... both Lord and Christ. (Acts 2:36)

Many Christians treat making Jesus Lord of their life as entirely optional. It is not. According to their line of reasoning, one may receive Jesus as Savior from sin, from death and eternal punishment, but leave off the Lord of Life and Master part. This is sort of like buying into Christ for the "fire insurance" He offers, but rejecting Him as boss of our earthly lives. We must confess Jesus as our LORD.

If you read through the Gospels you will quickly see that the credentials of Jesus Christ do not stop with Savior. He went beyond the cross and the empty tomb to the throne. He ascended into Heaven and was given dominion to reign as King forever. And until we make Jesus in our lives <u>right now</u> what He is in the universe forever, and that is Lord and Ruler of all, then we have not gone as far as we can.

I like the way a Christian quarterback once explained Jesus as Lord of his Life. He said, "Christ calls the plays. I run them." Are you willing to trust God to call the plays in your life starting right now? Are you willing to obey His word regarding finances, marriage, worship, child rearing, leisure, giving, prayer, and forgiveness? Are you willing to let Jesus rule your life? He is Christ and Lord!

My Quiet Time Journal

1.   Ready yourself for a Fresh encounter with God. Pray and ask God to speak to you. (Psalm 37:7)

2.   Read the Scripture of the Day and prepare to hear a **Fresh Word** from God. (II Timothy 3:16-17)

3.   Respond with the *"Mind of Christ"* by writing down what God has said to you through the Scripture and the devotional thoughts. (Jeremiah 33:3)

4.   Reflect as you *"Experience God"* by listening to His Voice and writing down your prayers and thoughts. (John 16:23)

5.   Rely on Jesus to help you live out these truths. (Luke 11:28) Ask, *"Lord, what do you want me to do today?"*   (God's to-do list.)

(Pray for strength as you put on the Full Armor of God.)

Acts 2:37-41

The Results Were Startling

Peter preached a crucified and risen Christ, supporting what he said with Scripture. The results were startling: "When the people heard this, they were cut to the heart and said to Peter and the other Apostles, Brothers, what shall we do?" (Acts 2:37) The first question the people asked was "What does this mean?" (Acts 2:12) Their second question was "What shall we do?" When people see God working in the lives of His people, they want to understand. In response to the first question, Peter said, "Let me explain this to you." - and he shared the Gospel of Jesus Christ. As the Gospel was shared in the power of the Holy Spirit of God, people were convicted of their need, "they were cut to the heart," and they wanted to know what they needed to do.

What a great privilege it is to work with God in sharing with others what He is doing and has done for us. Peter shares how they can be saved.

In this passage he says, "Repent and be baptized." In Acts 3:19 he says, "Repent and turn to God." In Acts 16:31, Paul tells the jailer, "Believe in the Lord Jesus, and you will be saved."

Salvation is based on what Christ did for us and our acceptance. Repentance is turning away from our sin and turning to God through Jesus. Baptism shows our acceptance and faith in Christ by saying to others, "I'm following Christ." The old self is dead and buried and we have arisen to newness of life.

My Quiet Time Journal

1.   **Ready yourself** for a Fresh encounter with God. Pray and ask God to speak to you. (Psalm 37:7)

2.   **Read** the Scripture of the Day and prepare to hear a **Fresh Word** from God. (II Timothy 3:16-17)

3.   **Respond** with the **"Mind of Christ"** by writing down what God has said to you through the Scripture and the devotional thoughts. (Jeremiah 33:3)

4.   **Reflect** as you **"Experience God"** by listening to His Voice and writing down your prayers and thoughts. (John 16:23)

5.   **Rely** on Jesus to help you live out these truths. (Luke 11:28) Ask, **"Lord, what do you want me to do today?"**   (God's to-do list.)

(Pray for strength as you put on the Full Armor of God.)

Acts 2:42-47

The Foundation of Christian Discipleship

Let's look at Acts 2:42: "They devoted themselves to the Apostles' teaching and to fellowship, to the breaking of bread and to prayer." Here is an inside look at the genesis of Christian fellowship. Here is the foundation of Christian discipleship. Here's the original design. What a resource for those who want to follow the New Testament pattern of discipleship! What are some of the characteristics we see?

For one thing, these believers were teachable. They were eager and ready to learn. They devoted themselves to the Apostles' teaching. They were not doubters, they were believers. They were responsive individuals, not critical spirits. An eagerness to learn, a teachable spirit, is one of the master keys to usefulness in the cause of Christ.

Next, we see that they also devoted themselves to fellowship, to the breaking of bread, and to prayer. Fellowship here is so much more than getting together once in a while. The disciples came together frequently and shared their very lives with one another. Coming together in small groups seems to be part of the answer to having this type of fellowship, but we must go farther. It seems that these disciples craved intimacy with God and with their brothers and sister in Christ! Day by day they continued with one mind (unity) in the temple, and broke bread from house to house. How important it is to get together with brothers and sisters in Christ to encourage and help one another. How wonderful it is to have friends to share what we questioning or struggling with. It is a blessing.

My Quiet Time Journal

1. **Ready yourself** for a Fresh encounter with God. Pray and ask God to speak to you. (Psalm 37:7)

2. **Read** the Scripture of the Day and prepare to hear a **Fresh Word** from God. (II Timothy 3:16-17)

3. **Respond** with the *"Mind of Christ"* by writing down what God has said to you through the Scripture and the devotional thoughts. (Jeremiah 33:3)

4. **Reflect** as you *"Experience God"* by listening to His Voice and writing down your prayers and thoughts. (John 16:23)

5. **Rely** on Jesus to help you live out these truths. (Luke 11:28) Ask, *"Lord, what do you want me to do today?"*   (God's to-do list.)

(Pray for strength as you put on the Full Armor of God.)

The Foundation of Christian Discipleship
(Part II)

These disciples were worshipful. The fellowship of the Lord's Supper, prayers, and praise were an integral part of their lives. Churches today often wish that some of the early Christian's spirit of worship would catch fire in our assemblies. The elements of worship may be present, but it is all in vain if our minds are wandering, our hearts are set on other things, and our spirits are cold. We have a great heritage, a great foundation. We need the touch of God on our souls to restore us to the kind of heartfelt worship our ancestors in the faith practiced.

The early believers displayed another characteristic that is badly needed today: they were a glad people. Gladness is a powerful force for good in the world. There is healing and strength in a glad spirit. When you are with a glad person, you are helped and strengthened in many ways. The joy of the LORD becomes your strength through them.

The early Christians were also sacrificial. "All the believers were together and had everything in common. Selling their possessions and goods, they gave to anyone as he had need." (Acts 2:44-45) Why did they sacrifice for one another? Why did they spend time with one another? Why did the early disciples invest their lives in these new converts? Does not the love of God compel us to meet the needs of others? We know it does.

It seems to me that the answer is in the commission that Jesus had given. The commission was not just to get converts, but to make disciples. Teachers and Students.

My Quiet Time Journal

1.   Ready yourself for a Fresh encounter with God. Pray and ask God to speak to you. (Psalm 37:7)

2.   Read the Scripture of the Day and prepare to hear a **Fresh Word** from God. (II Timothy 3:16-17)

3.   Respond with the *"Mind of Christ"* by writing down what God has said to you through the Scripture and the devotional thoughts. (Jeremiah 33:3)

4.   Reflect as you *"Experience God"* by listening to His Voice and writing down your prayers and thoughts. (John 16:23)

5.   Rely on Jesus to help you live out these truths. (Luke 11:28) Ask, *"Lord, what do you want me to do today?"*   (God's to-do list.)

(Pray for strength as you put on the Full Armor of God.)

Week Three - Day One

Acts 3:1

A Time for Prayer

Dr. Luke tells us "One day Peter and John were going up to the temple at the time of prayer - at three (ninth hour) in the afternoon." I believe if we don't have a time to pray, we will not have time to pray. This is not in contradiction to the teachings in the Bible "to pray without ceasing," but to enforce the attitude of prayer at all times so that we may enter into fervent prayer at specific times. Have you set a specific time for prayer and your daily devotion time?

Daniel had regular times of prayer which he kept even at the risk of his own life. "Now when Daniel learned that the decree had been published, he went home to his upstairs room where the windows opened toward Jerusalem. Three times a day, he got down on his knees and prayed, giving thanks to his God, just as he had done before." (Daniel 6:10) David said, "Every morning and noon I cry out in distress, and He hears my voice." (Psalm 55:17)

It is interesting to note than when Daniel prayed, in this instance, he was giving thanks to Almighty God. The verse in Psalms says that David cried out in distress - apparently asking for help. I think that sometimes our prayers are more for "asking" than for thanksgiving. Even though God knows all our needs before we ask, we need to make our needs known to God so we are aware of them also. We may not even know them until prompted by the Holy Spirit in prayer. Then the asking becomes a time of thanksgiving as God ministers to our needs. This week, continue to practice your praying.

My Quiet Time Journal

1. **Ready yourself** for a Fresh encounter with God. Pray and ask God to speak to you. (Psalm 37:7)

2. **Read** the Scripture of the Day and prepare to hear a **Fresh Word** from God. (II Timothy 3:16-17)

3. **Respond** with the *"Mind of Christ"* by writing down what God has said to you through the Scripture and the devotional thoughts. (Jeremiah 33:3)

4. **Reflect** as you *"Experience God"* by listening to His Voice and writing down your prayers and thoughts. (John 16:23)

5. **Rely** on Jesus to help you live out these truths. (Luke 11:28) Ask, *"Lord, what do you want me to do today?"*   (God's to-do list.)

(Pray for strength as you put on the Full Armor of God.)

Week Three - Day Two

Acts 3:2-4

Be Flexible

How many of us would stop to talk to a "beggar" on the street when we are on our way to church on Sunday morning? I think the answer is most of us want to help someone in need. Even though we have on clean clothes, and we don't want to get dirty, we would help if someone asked for help. The problem is that we don't go ask someone if they need help - we want to be on time to church. Peter and John took time to stop and look at him carefully, and then say to him "Look on us."

Flexibility was a part of the character of these two Apostles. I am sure that those years with Jesus had much to do with their outlook on life. If it wasn't a woman with a blood problem, it was a blind beggar calling out to the Son of David for mercy. Interruptions and changed plans were nothing new to the Apostles. It was a part of their daily life.

Why do we become so upset when things happen to change our plans? I think it is because we are so self-centered that we consider another person's problems not important enough to delay our immediate goals. The Bible teaches that we "are not our own, but we are bought with a price." (1 Corinthians 6:19-20)

We must set goals and maintain some order in our lives and have specific times for spiritual refreshing, but we cannot become rigid and inflexible. A rigid person may break under heavy loads in life, but a flexible person will bend under heavy loads and then bounce back. Discipleship always includes "positive flexibility".

My Quiet Time Journal

1.   Ready yourself for a Fresh encounter with God. Pray and ask God to speak to you. (Psalm 37:7)

2.   Read the Scripture of the Day and prepare to hear a **Fresh Word** from God. (II Timothy 3:16-17)

3.   Respond with the *"Mind of Christ"* by writing down what God has said to you through the Scripture and the devotional thoughts. (Jeremiah 33:3)

4.   Reflect as you *"Experience God"* by listening to His Voice and writing down your prayers and thoughts. (John 16:23)

5.   Rely on Jesus to help you live out these truths.(Luke 11:28) Ask, *"Lord, what do you want me to do today?"*   (God's to-do list.)

(Pray for strength as you put on the Full Armor of God.)

Acts 3:5-11

People Oriented

This account of Peter and John stopping to help a poor, lame man exemplifies what Christianity is all about. The beggar probably had more money than Peter and John, but the question of money never came up. Peter saw a more serious problem than material poverty, he saw spiritual poverty. In my lifetime, I have seen beggars on the street asking for money or selling something and hoping for a generous amount for their ware. I have always seen beggars positioned on corners, never at a church. I suppose the are all active seven days a week, as compared to the church, being active basically one day a week. Verse 6 speaks to me strongly because I will many times see many people giving the beggar something, but I never took the time to stop and help him spiritually. After having given someone money, you will go away feeling good, because God always blesses when we give out of compassion. However, we miss the greater blessings that come when spiritual gifts are shared. That is also discipleship.

I believe that the Holy Spirit directed Peter to call upon the healing powers of Heaven through Jesus to heal the man. The Scripture reveals that the man asks for money, not for healing. God wants the people who live today to know that God can and will perform miracles through his servants - Praise God! The man was not healed sitting down; only after Peter took him by the right hand and lifted him up, did his feet and ankles receive strength. I believe that we must "stand up" in faith for the impossible to be accomplished. It takes their desire also.

My Quiet Time Journal

1.   Ready yourself for a Fresh encounter with God. Pray and ask God to speak to you. (Psalm 37:7)

2.   Read the Scripture of the Day and prepare to hear a **Fresh Word** from God. (II Timothy 3:16-17)

3.   Respond with the *"Mind of Christ"* by writing down what God has said to you through the Scripture and the devotional thoughts. (Jeremiah 33:3)

4.   Reflect as you *"Experience God"* by listening to His Voice and writing down your prayers and thoughts. (John 16:23)

5.   Rely on Jesus to help you live out these truths. (Luke 11:28) Ask, *"Lord, what do you want me to do today?"*   (God's to-do list.)

(Pray for strength as you put on the Full Armor of God.)

Acts 3:12-16

Humility

After you read verses 12-16, read Acts 3:8 again. The healed man was so overcome with joy that he was jumping, running, and praising God. He was not giving himself any credit, nor was he giving Peter the credit for this miracle-only God. Many times when we receive a miracle of healing or protection, we will accredit everything and everyone but the Almighty God. "Good Luck" has been attributed with more miracles than God so it seems. But God wants all this Glory. He is God!

When Peter and John began to receive all the attention on Solomon's porch, I imagine they enjoyed it until they came back to reality of what God had really done. "And when Peter realize this he answered the people, "You men of Israel, why do you marvel at this? Or why do you look so earnestly on us, as though by our own power or holiness we made this man walk? (Acts 3:12) Peter was making a clear discipleship point.

If Peter and John had attempted to capitalize on what had happened, their ministry would have ended right there. However, instead of yielding to temptation, they obeyed the Holy Spirit and began to preach Jesus. Peter began by preaching, "The God of Abraham, and of Isaac, and of Jacob, the God of our fathers, has glorified His Son Jesus; whom you delivered up, and denied Him in the presence of Pilate, when he was determined to let Him go. (Acts 3:13) The focus was on making Jesus famous.

I wonder how many people would have listened to Peter preach on Solomon's porch if a miracle had not been performed. Perhaps some, but not as many as there were because they saw the crippled man running and praising God. But God was at work.

What does Humility look like to you? In all that you do for the LORD, are you looking to make Jesus famous? Is God at work?

My Quiet Time Journal

1. **Ready yourself** for a Fresh encounter with God. Pray and ask God to speak to you. (Psalm 37:7)

2. **Read** the Scripture of the Day and prepare to hear a **Fresh Word** from God. (II Timothy 3:16-17)

3. **Respond** with the *"Mind of Christ"* by writing down what God has said to you through the Scripture and the devotional thoughts. (Jeremiah 33:3)

4. **Reflect** as you *"Experience God"* by listening to His Voice and writing down your prayers and thoughts. (John 16:23)

5. **Rely** on Jesus to help you live out these truths. (Luke 11:28) Ask, *"Lord, what do you want me to do today?"* (God's to-do list.)

(Pray for strength as you put on the Full Armor of God.)

Week Three - Day Five

Acts 3:17-18

A Witnessing Opportunity

Peter began to witness for Jesus in a strong and mighty way. Peter was a reliable witness because he had seen the power of God demonstrated through Jesus. How can a Christian be a witness for Jesus if he has not seen Jesus perform a mighty work or miracle? In order for a person to be a credible witness in our civil courts, the person must have seen or heard things relevant to the case. They cannot testify as to their opinion, nor what they have heard someone else say. They must testify and relate their personal involvement in the case. So it is with the Christian. He cannot testify to the power of God unless he has experienced it. The greatest miracle available for everyone who asks is "new life in Christ." If you've been "born again" you've experienced this miracle. Think about it. When Peter lifted the lame man up, his legs were immediately straightened and healed. The man quickly started praising God and telling other people what God had done with Peter as His instrument. Sometimes God will require several operations and a period of time before healing is accomplished. God should be praised at the end of this extended healing period just the same as the fast-healing period. I've seen people healed after a long stay in the hospital, and they did not thank God, or the doctors or nurses for their recovery. They only complained about the cost of the hospital bill. Then I realize how often I have taken the blessings of God for granted and failed to thank Him. Peter was quick to acknowledge Jesus as the Great Physician and then preach the message to all who would listen. Take time now and Praise God for your blessings.

My Quiet Time Journal

1. **Ready yourself** for a Fresh encounter with God. Pray and ask God to speak to you. (Psalm 37:7)

2. **Read** the Scripture of the Day and prepare to hear a **Fresh Word** from God. (II Timothy 3:16-17)

3. **Respond** with the *"Mind of Christ"* by writing down what God has said to you through the Scripture and the devotional thoughts. (Jeremiah 33:3)

4. **Reflect** as you *"Experience God"* by listening to His Voice and writing down your prayers and thoughts. (John 16:23)

5. **Rely** on Jesus to help you live out these truths. (Luke 11:28) Ask, *"Lord, what do you want me to do today?"*   (God's to-do list.)

(Pray for strength as you put on the Full Armor of God.)

Week Three - Day Six

Acts 3:19-25

Repentance

Peter was preaching a new message brought into the world by Jesus. Jesus said "Unless you repent, you will all perish." (Luke 13:3) Peter said, "Repent, then, and turn to God, so that your sins may be wiped out, that times of refreshing may come from the Lord," (Acts 3:19) The old message of payment for sin through sacrificial offerings had been changed forever by Jesus. I am sure the people thought that this was too easy - that forgiveness of sin could be accomplished without giving up money. They had to learn that Jesus had paid the price for sins, and each person can appropriate the greatest of all sacrifices for their own salvation and release from sin. They would later learn that what they had to give was themselves to Christ.

Peter had to explain further to the people as to what was happening when he said, "For Moses said, 'The Lord your God will raise up for you a prophet like me from among your own people; you must listen to everything he tells you." (Acts 3:22) The Jews of that day, and also today, evaluate events in the light of Old Testament prophecy. If there is the slightest discrepancy between an event and prophecy, they will not accept the event as God's will. I believe that Satan is the author of doubt, and that Jesus is the author of faith and spiritual assurance. We must make sure our actions are substantiated by God's Truth in His Word.

My Quiet Time Journal

1.   Ready yourself for a Fresh encounter with God. Pray and ask God to speak to you. (Psalm 37:7)

2.   Read the Scripture of the Day and prepare to hear a **Fresh Word** from God. (II Timothy 3:16-17)

3.   Respond with the *"Mind of Christ"* by writing down what God has said to you through the Scripture and the devotional thoughts. (Jeremiah 33:3)

4.   Reflect as you *"Experience God"* by listening to His Voice and writing down your prayers and thoughts. (John 16:23)

5.   Rely on Jesus to help you live out these truths. (Luke 11:28) Ask, *"Lord, what do you want me to do today?"*   (God's to-do list.)

(Pray for strength as you put on the Full Armor of God.)

Week Three - Day Seven

Acts 3:26

Justification

Peter clearly explains that our "turning away from our wicked ways" was the perfect work of Christ. There is no inference that anything we have done, or can do, is a factor in our deliverance. The whole matter is summed up in one statement that "God raised up His Servant (Jesus) and sent Him to bless you."

There have been literally thousands of books written on how man can become worthy and "God-like" by following certain routines and practices. This is attempting to be justified before God by good works. That is religion. Paul clearly said that justification before God can only be obtained through Christ. "Know that a man is not justified by the work of the law, but by faith in Jesus Christ; that we might be justified by faith in Christ, and not by the works of the law; for by the works of the law shall no flesh be justified." (Galatians 2:16) That is by a relationship.

Many religions base their justification on the premise that if you do not do bad things you are good, and have the right to go to heaven. This is a deception of Satan based on human logic. Christianity bases our justification on a personal relationship with God through His Son the LORD Jesus Christ that God makes happen by the power of the Holy Spirit.

It seems to be strange but it is true that there will not be any good people in heaven - only saved people. Jesus said, "There is none good - no not one." and I believe Jesus. Our only chance of being saved is through God's Gift of Justification (Jesus). John 14:6. There is no other name given in which we can be saved. No other name, but the name of Jesus. He is the one who justifies.

My Quiet Time Journal

1. **Ready yourself** for a Fresh encounter with God. Pray and ask God to speak to you. (Psalm 37:7)

2. **Read** the Scripture of the Day and prepare to hear a **Fresh Word** from God. (II Timothy 3:16-17)

3. **Respond** with the *"Mind of Christ"* by writing down what God has said to you through the Scripture and the devotional thoughts. (Jeremiah 33:3)

4. **Reflect** as you *"Experience God"* by listening to His Voice and writing down your prayers and thoughts. (John 16:23)

5. **Rely** on Jesus to help you live out these truths. (Luke 11:28) Ask, *"Lord, what do you want me to do today?"*   (God's to-do list.)

(Pray for strength as you put on the Full Armor of God.)

Should we do any less?

When Jesus walked the earth, he was asked a question similar to the one the Sanhedrin asked Peter. "Jesus entered the temple courts, and, while he was teaching, the chief priests and the elders of the people came to him. 'By what authority are you doing these things?' They asked. 'And who gave you this authority?'" (Matthew 21:23). Jesus countered with another question. He asked the elders whether John's baptism came from heaven or from men. Since they would not answer his question directly, Jesus said he would not tell them by what authority he was teaching. After telling them two parables, Jesus concluded that conversation by saying, "Have you never read in the Scriptures: 'The stone the builders rejected has become the capstone; the Lord has done this, and it is marvelous in our eyes'?" (Matthew 21:42). Now notice Peter's response to his questioners: "He is 'the stone you builders rejected, which has become the chief corner stone'" (Acts 4:11).

This incident shows us the awesome power of example, Peter did just what Jesus had done. Jesus had cited Psalm 118:22 and so Peter did the same. This is a good lesson for us. Someone is watching us, someone is listening to us, just as Peter observed Jesus. That knowledge alone should keep us on the straight and narrow path. When he talks about a real Christian, he will be thinking of you. Therefore, what you do—the way you behave, the amusements you enjoy, how you spend your time, your activities—will be copied by someone. You are his example. That is true discipleship. In the situation recorded in Acts 4, Peter did exactly as Jesus had done. Should we do any less?

My Quiet Time Journal

1. **Ready yourself** for a Fresh encounter with God. Pray and ask God to speak to you. (Psalm 37:7)

2. **Read** the Scripture of the Day and prepare to hear a **Fresh Word** from God. (II Timothy 3:16-17)

3. **Respond** with the *"Mind of Christ"* by writing down what God has said to you through the Scripture and the devotional thoughts. (Jeremiah 33:3)

4. **Reflect** as you *"Experience God"* by listening to His Voice and writing down your prayers and thoughts. (John 16:23)

5. **Rely** on Jesus to help you live out these truths. (Luke 11:28) Ask, *"Lord, what do you want me to do today?"* (God's to-do list.)

(Pray for strength as you put on the Full Armor of God.)

No Other Name...But Jesus!

There is a consistency to Peter's messages throughout Acts. On the day of Pentecost he spoke about the death and resurrection of Jesus (Acts 2:23-24). He gave the same message to the crowd that gathered in Jerusalem (Acts 3:14-15). Now he gave the same message to the Sadducees: "let it be known to all of you and to all the people of Israel, that by the name of Jesus Christ the Nazarene-whom you crucified and whom God raised from the dead-by Him this man is standing here before you healthy."(Acts 4:10). Still later we find him repeating the same message to Cornelius: "We are witnesses of everything he did in the country of the Jews and in Jerusalem. They killed him by hanging him on a tree, but God raised him from the dead on the third day and caused him to be seen" (Acts 26:22-23)

Why did they always give this particular message? The answer is found in Paul's letter to the Corinthians: "Now, brothers, I want to remind you of the gospel I preached to you, which you received and on which you have taken your stand. By this gospel you are saved, if you hold firmly to the word I preached to you. Otherwise, you have believed in vain. For what I received I passed on to you as first importance: that Christ died for our sins according to the Scriptures, and that he was buried, that he was raised on the third day according to the Scriptures" (1Corinthians 15:1-4). This is the gospel. This is the good news. Jesus explicitly told his followers to "preach the good news to all creation" (Mark 16:15). Peter, and all the other apostles, obeyed his command. Peter gave a firm, clear, ringing witness to the uniqueness of our Lord Jesus Christ. "There is salvation in no one else, for there is no other name under heaven given to people by which we must be saved." (Acts 4:12).

Other religions can tell us what we ought to be. Christ *transforms* us into what we ought to be. Other religions make us *aware* of our needs. Christ *meets* our needs.

My Quiet Time Journal

1.   Ready yourself for a Fresh encounter with God. Pray and ask God to speak to you. (Psalm 37:7)

2.   Read the Scripture of the Day and prepare to hear a **Fresh Word** from God. (II Timothy 3:16-17)

3.   Respond with the *"Mind of Christ"* by writing down what God has said to you through the Scripture and the devotional thoughts. (Jeremiah 33:3)

4.   Reflect as you *"Experience God"* by listening to His Voice and writing down your prayers and thoughts. (John 16:23)

5.   Rely on Jesus to help you live out these truths. (Luke 11:28) Ask, *"Lord, what do you want me to do today?"*   (God's to-do list.)

(Pray for strength as you put on the Full Armor of God.)

Acts 4:23-31

"Under the Influence"

Acts 4:31 says that "After they prayed, the place where they were meeting was shaken. And they were all filled with the Holy Spirit and spoke the word of God boldly." What does it mean that they were "filled with the Holy Spirit"?

The apostle Paul gave a clear command: "Do not get drunk on wine, which leads to debauchery. Instead, be filled with the Spirit" (Ephesians 5:18). The Greek word for filled is *pleroo*, which means "to control." When we look carefully at the tense of the verbs, the sentence reads "Be continually controlled by the Spirit." Paul cites that as an alternative to being drunk with wine. When a person has had too much liquor, we say he is "under the influence." The liquor is in control. When he makes a fool of himself with some outlandish comment, we say the wine is speaking. We give the man the benefit of the doubt—if he was sober he would not talk like that. So Paul said we should continually be under the controlling influence of the Holy Spirit. And how does that take place? If you read and compare Ephesians 5:18 to 6:7 with Colossians 3:16-3:23, you will discover many parallel truths. In Ephesians Paul exhorts the believers to be filled with the Spirit. He urges the Colossians to be filled with the word.

Is there a difference? The answer is found in the teaching of Christ. Jesus said, "The Spirit gives life; the flesh counts nothing. The words I have spoken to you are spirit and they are life" (John 6:63). Did you catch that? His words are Spirit. If we want to be under the constant control of the Holy Spirit, we must live in daily obedience to the word of God. That was Peter's experience, and the Spirit used him mightily to proclaim the gospel of Christ.

My Quiet Time Journal

1. **Ready yourself** for a Fresh encounter with God. Pray and ask God to speak to you. (Psalm 37:7)

2. **Read** the Scripture of the Day and prepare to hear a **Fresh Word** from God. (II Timothy 3:16-17)

3. **Respond** with the *"Mind of Christ"* by writing down what God has said to you through the Scripture and the devotional thoughts. (Jeremiah 33:3)

4. **Reflect** as you *"Experience God"* by listening to His Voice and writing down your prayers and thoughts. (John 16:23)

5. **Rely** on Jesus to help you live out these truths. (Luke 11:28) Ask, *"Lord, what do you want me to do today?"* (God's to-do list.)

(Pray for strength as you put on the Full Armor of God.)

"Teamwork"

We should note two important reasons for the success of these early believers recorded in Acts 4:32. "Now the multitude of those who believed were of one heart and soul, and no one said that any of his possessions was his own, but instead they held everything in common." Two lessons can be drawn from this verse. The first is <u>unity</u>. The early Christians put forth a united witness. They were one in heart, soul, spirit, and mind. The second is <u>sacrifice</u>. They were willing to give whatever it took to get the job done. They gave their lives, their money, their time, their all. They did not hold back. Sacrifice was part of their lifestyle. Jesus had shown the way and they followed him gladly.

The team work of the two who were the main actors in the drama of Acts 4–Peter and John—is another evidence of the power of God to blend men's hearts together and to unite them as a team. Here was Peter—impulsive, straightforward, a decisive man of action. And here was John—the disciple of love. But under the control of the Holy Spirit there was no conflict. So the apostles were united and the people were united. Their teamwork contributed to a great and powerful witness for Christ that changed their world, and which continues to change our world to this very day.

Evidence of their sacrificial spirit is found in Acts 4:34-37: " For there was not a needy person among them, because all those who owned lands or houses sold them, brought the proceeds of the things that were sold, and laid them at the apostles' feet. This was then distributed to each person as anyone had a need. Joseph, a Levite and a Cypriot by birth, whom the apostles named Barnabas, which is translated Son of Encouragement, sold a field he owned, brought the money, and laid it at the apostles' feet."

My Quiet Time Journal

1.   Ready yourself for a Fresh encounter with God. Pray and ask God to speak to you. (Psalm 37:7)

2.   Read the Scripture of the Day and prepare to hear a **Fresh Word** from God. (II Timothy 3:16-17)

3.   Respond with the **"Mind of Christ"** by writing down what God has said to you through the Scripture and the devotional thoughts. (Jeremiah 33:3)

4.   Reflect as you **"Experience God"** by listening to His Voice and writing down your prayers and thoughts. (John 16:23)

5.   Rely on Jesus to help you live out these truths. (Luke 11:28) Ask, **"Lord, what do you want me to do today?"**   (God's to-do list.)

(Pray for strength as you put on the Full Armor of God.)

Acts 5:1-11

"Did the Devil 'make' you do it?"

There are two key lessons in these verses. One is the danger of hypocrisy. Jesus dealt very tenderly with open sinners, but bluntly condemned all hypocrites. I must not brag about things I haven't done. Nor must I promise to do something and then fail to do it. "When you make a vow to God, do not delay in fulfilling it. He has no pleasure in fools; fulfill your vow. It is better not to vow than to make a vow and not fulfill it" (Ecclesiastes 5:4-5). The Holy Spirit is also known as the Spirit of truth, so a person who is led by the Spirit will tell the truth. As a follower of Christ, I must tell the truth. The second key lesson is one of encouragement for us. Notice Acts 5:3-4:

"Then Peter said, "Ananias, why has Satan filled your heart to lie to the Holy Spirit and keep back part of the proceeds from the field? Wasn't it yours while you possessed it? And after it was sold, wasn't it at your disposal? Why is it that you planned this thing in your heart? You have not lied to men but to God!"

Satan can tempt me to sin, but not force me into it. It is always my decision. In the process God always provides an alternative. When a temptation comes slinking up, a way of escape comes marching alongside. I then evaluate the two and make a decision. "No temptation has seized you except what is common to man. And God is faithful; he will not let you be tempted beyond what you can bear. But when you are tempted, he will also provide a way out so that you can stand up under it" (1 Corinthians 10:13). So we cannot place the blame on the devil. He can tempt us, but that is all he can do. God has placed him within some limits. We can never truthfully say, "the devil made me do it."

My Quiet Time Journal

1.   Ready yourself for a Fresh encounter with God. Pray and ask God to speak to you. (Psalm 37:7)

2.   Read the Scripture of the Day and prepare to hear a **Fresh Word** from God. (II Timothy 3:16-17)

3.   Respond with the *"Mind of Christ"* by writing down what God has said to you through the Scripture and the devotional thoughts. (Jeremiah 33:3)

4.   Reflect as you *"Experience God"* by listening to His Voice and writing down your prayers and thoughts. (John 16:23)

5.   Rely on Jesus to help you live out these truths. (Luke 11:28) Ask, *"Lord, what do you want me to do today?"*   (God's to-do list.)

(Pray for strength as you put on the Full Armor of God.)

Week Four – Day Six

Acts 5:12-16

"Seeing with the eyes of Jesus"

The apostles knew they were in danger. Why didn't they flee or hide? For one simple reason: they had been told to witness. So they witnessed. We have been given the same command, Peter wrote, "But you are chosen people, a royal priesthood, a holy nation, a people belonging to God, that you may declare the praises of him who called you out of darkness into his wonderful light" (1 Peter 2:9). What does it take to have a witnessing lifestyle? To make witnessing a regular, normal, and vital part of our lives, we need to *see things as Jesus saw them*. When he saw the crowds, he had compassion on them, because they were harassed and helpless, like sheep without a shepherd. Then he said to his disciples, 'The harvest is plentiful but the workers are few. Ask the Lord of the harvest, therefore, to send our workers into his harvest field'" (Matthew 9:36-38).

Jesus saw the harvest as plentiful. He also spoke about the harvest on another occasion. "Do you not say, 'Four months more and then the harvest'? I tell you, open your eyes and look at the fields! They are ripe for harvest" (John 4:35). He said the harvest is ready to be gathered in.

Is that the way you see things? When you look at the world about you, do you see a vast, overripe harvest? When you look at your neighborhood, do you see those that don't know Jesus as their Lord and Savior?

My Quiet Time Journal

1. **Ready yourself** for a Fresh encounter with God. Pray and ask God to speak to you. (Psalm 37:7)

2. **Read** the Scripture of the Day and prepare to hear a **Fresh Word** from God. (II Timothy 3:16-17)

3. **Respond** with the **"Mind of Christ"** by writing down what God has said to you through the Scripture and the devotional thoughts. (Jeremiah 33:3)

4. **Reflect** as you **"Experience God"** by listening to His Voice and writing down your prayers and thoughts. (John 16:23)

5. **Rely** on Jesus to help you live out these truths. (Luke 11:28) Ask, **"Lord, what do you want me to do today?"**   (God's to-do list.)

(Pray for strength as you put on the Full Armor of God.)

Acts 5:17-42

"Every Heart Without Christ is a Mission Field"

After the Sanhedrin learned the apostles were preaching in the temple courts, they sent the captain of the temple guard with his officers to bring the apostles before the council. Then the high priest said, "Didn't we strictly order you not to teach in this name? And look, you have filled Jerusalem with your teaching and are determined to bring this man's blood on us!" (Acts 5:28).

We can see in this account that Peter and the other apostles were compelled to speak out. They had a missionary mentality that should serve as an example for each of us. Every heart without Christ is a mission field. Every heart with Christ is a missionary. One of the great sources of power in the New Testament church was that they did not rely on a few "superstars" to do the ministry. In fact, when persecution came and they fled for their lives, even that did not quench their bold witness for Christ. "Those who had been scattered preached the word wherever they went" (Acts 8:4). Those who were scattered were ordinary believers. Philip, the table waiter, had a missionary mentality. When the Lord brought Philip in touch with "an Ethiopian eunuch, an important official in charge of all the treasury of Candace, queen of the Ethiopians" (Acts 8:27), Philip responded naturally, since the Ethiopian was reading a passage from Isaiah: "Philip began with that very passage of Scripture and told him the good news about Jesus" (Acts 8:35).

We must view ourselves as the means for God to shed abroad his love in the world by the Holy Spirit. Sharing the gospel is not optional for missionaries. Far too often we think of the missionary as someone who is "way out there." Admittedly, we must continue to have missionaries "way out there," but we must also have them "back here"—in the bank, garage, supermarket, office, and neighborhood. We're elected—we're to be those missionaries! God has appointed us to this task.

My Quiet Time Journal

1.   Ready yourself for a Fresh encounter with God. Pray and ask God to speak to you. (Psalm 37:7)

2.   Read the Scripture of the Day and prepare to hear a **Fresh Word** from God. (II Timothy 3:16-17)

3.   Respond with the **"Mind of Christ"** by writing down what God has said to you through the Scripture and the devotional thoughts. (Jeremiah 33:3)

4.   Reflect as you **"Experience God"** by listening to His Voice and writing down your prayers and thoughts. (John 16:23)

5.   Rely on Jesus to help you live out these truths. (Luke 11:28) Ask, **"Lord, what do you want me to do today?"**   (God's to-do list.)

(Pray for strength as you put on the Full Armor of God.)

Growing Pains

Growth, in any kind of group, will bring with it diversity – differing viewpoints, tastes, backgrounds, education, etc. While this in itself is good, people tend to be afraid of what they are ignorant of (prejudice).

It seems that the early church was no exception. God's church was growing, and we can be sure that Satan was not pleased. With any move of God comes opposition. This time the enemy's plan was to divide and conquer. As the Church grew with Jews that believed in Jesus they were divided into two groups. The first group were those who had remained in Judea, near Jerusalem, and spoke Hebrew. They were called Hebraic Jews. The second group consisted of those Jews who were scattered among the Gentiles, who spoke Greek, and who used the Greek translation of the Old Testament, called the Septuagint. They were called "Hellenists," from a word meaning "Greek-speaking."

The Palestinian or Hebraic Jews were proud of the fact that they had always lived in the land of the patriarchs and that they used the language that their forefathers spoke. They lived near the temple and worshiped there. On the other hand, the Hellenistic Jews from other parts of the world were jealous of the first group and made to feel like outsiders. Thus divisions arose between the Hellenistic Jews and the Hebraic Jews.

The complaint that arose was legitimate. The response of the church is what will be either to her credit or to her shame

My Quiet Time Journal

1.   Ready yourself for a Fresh encounter with God. Pray and ask God to speak to you. (Psalm 37:7)

2.   Read the Scripture of the Day and prepare to hear a **Fresh Word** from God. (II Timothy 3:16-17)

3.   Respond with the *"Mind of Christ"* by writing down what God has said to you through the Scripture and the devotional thoughts. (Jeremiah 33:3)

4.   Reflect as you *"Experience God"* by listening to His Voice and writing down your prayers and thoughts. (John 16:23)

5.   Rely on Jesus to help you live out these truths. (Luke 11:28) Ask, *"Lord, what do you want me to do today?"*   (God's to-do list.)

(Pray for strength as you put on the Full Armor of God.)

Acts 6:1-4

Word & Deed

The complaint had arisen. Either to ignore it or refute it would have caused division, clearly not the answer our Lord wants for His Bride, the Church. The Disciples had not forgotten Jesus' High Priestly prayer that "...they would be one, just as You and I are one." (John 17:22).

The Twelve chose not to neglect the Word of God in order to serve tables. However, to do one and not the other would have led to a seriously weakened church. Anytime the Word of God goes into the believer, it should work itself back out in Christian service. "For by grace you have been saved through faith; and that not of yourselves, it is a gift of God; not as a result of work, that no one should boast. For we are His workmanship, created in Christ Jesus for good works"... (Ephesians 2:8-10). Service without the Word of God loses its power. Devotion to the Word without service loses it's credibility and is dead. (James 2:17).

The First Deacons

We might be tempted for a moment to think that the Apostles had somehow thought that doing the dishes and serving tables was beneath them. However, it is unlikely that they would so forget that their Lord, the Creator of heaven and earth, had not too long ago washed their feet in a certain upper room. God at His core is a Servant, but not our "divine waiter," mind you! Yet, it is He who seeks after us! It is He that came and humbled Himself and gave. The Apostles were Spirit-filled men however, and knew God's specific call on their lives. Following the example of Moses in Exodus 18:21-25, they chose faithful men, wise and full of the Spirit, to put in charge of the task...our first Deacons.

My Quiet Time Journal

1.   Ready yourself for a Fresh encounter with God. Pray and ask God to speak to you. (Psalm 37:7)

2.   Read the Scripture of the Day and prepare to hear a **Fresh Word** from God. (II Timothy 3:16-17)

3.   Respond with the *"Mind of Christ"* by writing down what God has said to you through the Scripture and the devotional thoughts. (Jeremiah 33:3)

4.   Reflect as you *"Experience God"* by listening to His Voice and writing down your prayers and thoughts. (John 16:23)

5.   Rely on Jesus to help you live out these truths. (Luke 11:28) Ask, *"Lord, what do you want me to do today?"*   (God's to-do list.)

(Pray for strength as you put on the Full Armor of God.)

Acts 6:1-7

Diversity, yet Unified

In Christ we are one. He has knocked down the spiritual dividing wall between God and man. Therefore, if we are living in His presence and walking in His light, the dividing walls between man and fellow man will not be able to stand!

In Acts 6:5 we read that the Apostle's statement found approval with the entire congregation. Surely this was the work of the Holy Spirit!

The congregation chose seven men. Of these men, it was required that they be of good reputation, full of the Spirit, and full of wisdom. A man named Stephen headed the list. His was probably the first name off of everyone's tongue. The seven men all had Greek names, which seems to show they were probably from the Hellenist group to show that the Church was sensitive to the needs of the widows. That definitely showed some wisdom.

The newly selected deacons were brought before the Apostles and commissioned with prayer and the laying on of hands. This shows that they saw this position as spiritual, as well as, practical. The result was glorious! The Word of God continued to spread, the number of disciples continued to increase greatly, and many priests became obedient to the faith.

My Quiet Time Journal

1. **Ready yourself** for a Fresh encounter with God. Pray and ask God to speak to you. (Psalm 37:7)

2. **Read** the Scripture of the Day and prepare to hear a **Fresh Word** from God. (II Timothy 3:16-17)

3. **Respond** with the *"Mind of Christ"* by writing down what God has said to you through the Scripture and the devotional thoughts. (Jeremiah 33:3)

4. **Reflect** as you *"Experience God"* by listening to His Voice and writing down your prayers and thoughts. (John 16:23)

5. **Rely** on Jesus to help you live out these truths. (Luke 11:28) Ask, *"Lord, what do you want me to do today?"* (God's to-do list.)

(Pray for strength as you put on the Full Armor of God.)

Acts 6:8

Grace

"Stephen, full of grace and power, was performing great wonders and signs among the people." (Acts 6:8).

Looking at the Gospel of Luke, we find that Jesus is described as having the grace of God upon him (Luke 2:40) and as growing in grace with God and man (Luke 2:52). Now here in the Book of Acts we see many more references. Luke compares and contrasts grace and power, (4:33 ; 6:8 ; 11:23). Grace is also found in the phrases "message of his grace" (14:3), "grace of God" (14:26), "grace of our Lord Jesus" (15:11), and "grace of the Lord" (15:40). Luke is seeking it seems to make a statement about the deity of Christ and all of these phrases seemed to be linked with the power of God to create spiritual life and to sustain Christians. This grace is, as in the Old Testament passages, an unmerited favor, but now a new aspect of power in the Spirit has been added to it.

Paul, along with other New Testament writers in their salutations, always write "Grace and peace be unto you." Without grace, there is no power. Without grace we will have no peace. Without grace we will not be saved. Grace, God's Riches At Christ's Expense. You can't buy it, work for it, be good enough or cleave enough for it, or obtain it any way other than by asking for it from Jesus, who still give freely to all who will believe. Do you want His peace? Do you want His power? Let His grace and His Word abide in your richly! (Colossians 3:16).

My Quiet Time Journal

1. **Ready yourself** for a Fresh encounter with God. Pray and ask God to speak to you. (Psalm 37:7)

2. **Read** the Scripture of the Day and prepare to hear a **Fresh Word** from God. (II Timothy 3:16-17)

3. **Respond** with the *"Mind of Christ"* by writing down what God has said to you through the Scripture and the devotional thoughts. (Jeremiah 33:3)

4. **Reflect** as you *"Experience God"* by listening to His Voice and writing down your prayers and thoughts. (John 16:23)

5. **Rely** on Jesus to help you live out these truths. (Luke 11:28) Ask, *"Lord, what do you want me to do today?"* (God's to-do list.)

(Pray for strength as you put on the Full Armor of God.)

Acts 6:8-15

War and Peace

Stephen was dynamic! He was full of Grace and Power. He was, quite simply, full of Jesus! Jesus, though He is the Prince of Peace, says of Himself that He came to bring not peace, but a sword. (Matthew 10:35).

Apparently, the sword of Jesus had touched a sensitive area for a certain group of men. They rose up to argue, but were unable to cope with the wisdom and the Spirit with which Stephen was speaking. His enemies were now at a crossroads. They either had to admit that Stephen was speaking truth to them, and therefore humble themselves and repent, or take the low road and persecute him.

It is ironic that these men, in order to bring Stephen down, had to utterly shatter the commandments of God. The same commandments which they masqueraded to be keepers of they now were rejecting. It was a demonic display! But did they really bring Stephen down. No more so than death could keep Jesus in the grave! So now we are seeing the power of God displayed in the witness of a man who had committed his life to living for Jesus.

My Quiet Time Journal

1.   Ready yourself for a Fresh encounter with God. Pray and ask God to speak to you. (Psalm 37:7)

2.   Read the Scripture of the Day and prepare to hear a **Fresh Word** from God. (II Timothy 3:16-17)

3.   Respond with the *"Mind of Christ"* by writing down what God has said to you through the Scripture and the devotional thoughts. (Jeremiah 33:3)

4.   Reflect as you *"Experience God"* by listening to His Voice and writing down your prayers and thoughts. (John 16:23)

5.   Rely on Jesus to help you live out these truths. (Luke 11:28) Ask, *"Lord, what do you want me to do today?"*   (God's to-do list.)

(Pray for strength as you put on the Full Armor of God.)

Acts 6:15 – Acts 7:1-60

The Waiter

"Are these things so?" the high priest asks. (Acts 7:1).

Stephen's response would probably not have worked in today's courtroom setting. "Just answer the question," I can hear the judge say.   Stephen, however, appealed to his accusers as "brothers and fathers!" (Acts 7:2). What grace! He met them where they were! They knew the law of God. Stephen knew the law of God. Ah, some common ground.

Stephen probably didn't know that he would be called upon to preach that day, let alone what his text would be. Like King David of old, however, the Word of God was hid in his heart (Psalm 119:11). Stephen, not Reverend Stephen or Dr. Stephen or Apostle Stephen, but Stephen the one who waited on tables, launched into the history of the Jews. Had his accusers for a moment forgotten what they were there for, they would have had to let out an "Amen!" a few times in this most eloquent sermon. However, this was not to be. He did not end his sermon the way one might be taught at seminary. He did not water anything down. He would not be asked back next year to preach revival services. Again, in verses 51-54 the Sword of the Spirit strikes at the heart of the matter. This was not God's wrath, but God's love wooing them to come to the Savior and find forgiveness and salvation. Their hearts were cold from years of saying NO to God, and from their cold hearts came a crime most foul – the death of Stephen – the first martyr of the church!

My Quiet Time Journal

1.   **Ready yourself** for a Fresh encounter with God. Pray and ask God to speak to you. (Psalm 37:7)

2.   **Read** the Scripture of the Day and prepare to hear a **Fresh Word** from God. (II Timothy 3:16-17)

3.   **Respond** with the **"Mind of Christ"** by writing down what God has said to you through the Scripture and the devotional thoughts. (Jeremiah 33:3)

4.   **Reflect** as you **"Experience God"** by listening to His Voice and writing down your prayers and thoughts. (John 16:23)

5.   **Rely** on Jesus to help you live out these truths. (Luke 11:28) Ask, **"Lord, what do you want me to do today?"**   (God's to-do list.)

(Pray for strength as you put on the Full Armor of God.)

Look Unto Jesus

What comes out of you when you are bumped? If you have an appointment with an unpleasant person, you can brace yourself and try to put on a brave face. However, it's the "bump" from your blind side that will cause what is truly inside of you to spill out! Is what spills out of you a "blessing" or a "cursing?"

Stephen was full of Jesus. At his death he sees the heavens opened. He sees his Savior, and just as Jesus at His death offered forgiveness to His malefactors, Stephen, being full of the Holy Spirit, could do no other. "Lord, do not hold this sin against them!" (Acts 7:60). Stephen offered up two short prayers in his dying moments. Though the sin was very great, yet if they would lay it to their hearts, God would not lay it to their charge. Stephen died as much in a hurry as ever any man did, yet, when he died, the words used are, he fell asleep; he applied himself to his dying work with as much composure as if he had been going to sleep.

Witnessing the brutal murder of Stephen was Saul of Tarsus. This time, he looked on with approval. Later, he would come to know the grace and peace that only Jesus can give. Later, the persecutor would become the persecuted, and would gladly give up his own life for the Gospel!

Are we looking to Jesus as we serve Him no matter what? Are we teaching this truth to the next Generation?

My Quiet Time Journal

1.   **Ready yourself** for a Fresh encounter with God. Pray and ask God to speak to you. (Psalm 37:7)

2.   **Read** the Scripture of the Day and prepare to hear a **Fresh Word** from God. (II Timothy 3:16-17)

3.   **Respond** with the *"Mind of Christ"* by writing down what God has said to you through the Scripture and the devotional thoughts. (Jeremiah 33:3)

4.   **Reflect** as you *"Experience God"* by listening to His Voice and writing down your prayers and thoughts. (John 16:23)

5.   **Rely** on Jesus to help you live out these truths. (Luke 11:28) Ask, *"Lord, what do you want me to do today?"*   (God's to-do list.)

(Pray for strength as you put on the Full Armor of God.)

Week Six- Day One

Acts 8:1-4

Scattered

Satan's strategy was to destroy the church from without by persecution. His chief agent was a young, zealous Pharisee-- Saul of Tarsus. It was Saul's mission to destroy this doctrine that threatened Judaism. Saul dragged believers out of their homes and had them imprisoned. He put some to death (22:4). He tried to compel some believers to blaspheme (26:11). This persecution caused the church to spread from Jerusalem into Judea and Samaria. This fulfilled Christ's command to be His witnesses beyond the borders of Jerusalem (Acts 1:8). Believers are to go all over the world testifying of the glorious grace of God bestowed through His Son, Jesus the Living Christ. Each of us know the Great Commission (Matt. 28:19-20). Yet, we get complacent and lazy. It took persecution to get the first church into compliance with God's will. What will it take to motivate us?

The church was "scattered" (verse 1,4). This word is an agricultural term referring to the sowing of seed. Jesus tells us in Matthew 13:37-38 that He is the Sower and the good seed are His children of the Kingdom. These scattered believers preached the word of God everywhere they went, amidst persecution. Instead of fear, they had faith and fruit. Are you a good seed bearing fruit?

We have been blessed with freedom to worship Jesus openly and to study His Word. But, what would happen if your life, family, or freedom were threatened if you did not disown Jesus? One day, there may be a line drawn in the sand. Have you counted the cost of being Jesus' disciple?

My Quiet Time Journal

1. **Ready yourself** for a Fresh encounter with God. Pray and ask God to speak to you. (Psalm 37:7)

2. Read the Scripture of the Day and prepare to hear a **Fresh Word** from God. (II Timothy 3:16-17)

3. **Respond** with the *"Mind of Christ"* by writing down what God has said to you through the Scripture and the devotional thoughts. (Jeremiah 33:3)

4. **Reflect** as you *"Experience God"* by listening to His Voice and writing down your prayers and thoughts. (John 16:23)

5. **Rely** on Jesus to help you live out these truths. (Luke 11:28) Ask, *"Lord, what do you want me to do today?"* (God's to-do list.)

(Pray for strength as you put on the Full Armor of God.)

Love the Unlovable

Philip the table server (servant) goes to Samaria to preach Jesus to them. He is obeying Christ's command to carry the Gospel to Samaria (Acts 1:8). There was a deep hatred and bigotry between the Jews and the Samaritans. Jews considered them as "half-breeds" and "dogs." Yet, Jesus loved them (John 4) and died for them also. Philip, bearing the Holy Spirit's fruit, was allowing Jesus to love the unlovable through him. God loves all men and desires for none to perish. How then can we keep such great news to ourselves? Many Samaritans believed Philip's preaching when they saw mighty miracles accomplished. A sorcerer, Simon, "believed" with his intellect but had no "heart" faith. His focus was on the Holy Spirit's miracles and how this could exalt himself. He had not acknowledged his own sinfulness, repented, and appropriated Jesus as his personal Lord and Savior. Peter's reference to Simon's bitterness and bondage to sin may relate to the apostasy described in Deut. 29:18. Satan tries to dilute, delude, and destroy the church from within by sowing counterfeits ("tares") amidst the good seed. It was necessary for two reasons that Peter and John lay hands on the new believers at this formative stage of the church. First Jesus, had given Peter "the keys to the Kingdom of heaven" (Matt. 16:19); the privilege to open the door of faith to others). Peter had already used these keys at Pentecost for the Jews. Second, it was necessary that this new church in Samaria be identified in unity with the church in Jerusalem (John 17:21; Eph. 4:4-6). "Behold, how good and how pleasant it is for brethren to dwell together in unity!" (Psalm 133:1).

My Quiet Time Journal

1. **Ready yourself** for a Fresh encounter with God. Pray and ask God to speak to you. (Psalm 37:7)

2. **Read** the Scripture of the Day and prepare to hear a **Fresh Word** from God. (II Timothy 3:16-17)

3. **Respond** with the *"Mind of Christ"* by writing down what God has said to you through the Scripture and the devotional thoughts. (Jeremiah 33:3)

4. **Reflect** as you *"Experience God"* by listening to His Voice and writing down your prayers and thoughts. (John 16:23)

5. **Rely** on Jesus to help you live out these truths. (Luke 11:28) Ask, *"Lord, what do you want me to do today?"* (God's to-do list.)

(Pray for strength as you put on the Full Armor of God.)

Acts 8:26-40

How Can They Know? Unless ...

God twice gives Philip specific instructions of what to do (verses 26,29). Philip is available, faithful, and obedient. He finds an Ethiopian eunuch that has traveled over 200 miles to worship in Jerusalem. Although the eunuch could not enter the Temple (Deut. 23:1), he saw lambs sacrificed. With this picture in his mind, he is confused by Isaiah 53. When we see God at work around us, we are invited (as was Philip) to join Him in His work. (John 5:19) The eunuch needed someone to explain the Word of God to him. The whole world is dying of such a need! "How then shall they call on Him in whom they have not heard? And how shall they hear without a preacher?" (Romans 10:14). Philip preached Jesus Christ, the Son of God to the eunuch. He expounded how this Lamb took away the sin of the world. He showed how this beautiful tender root became the Man or Sorrows - despised, acquainted with grief, stricken, smitten of God, and afflicted. This silent Lamb was slaughtered for our sin as He interceded for our transgressions. We have healing and peace with God because Jesus' blood sprinkled the Mercy Seat. There is life and love in Jesus Christ. Why don't we tell it then? The Holy Spirit in the book of Acts is mandating that we take the Gospel to the whole world. Is it not interesting that in chapters 8-10 that there is a conversion experience of a representative of each of the sons of Noah (who populated the whole earth after the flood)? (Chapter 8: Ethiopian - Ham; Chapter 9: Saul - Shem; Chapter 10: Cornelius - Japheth). Believer - WAKE UP! Jesus' return is near and so many are perishing! Generation next is waiting to hear.

My Quiet Time Journal

1.   **Ready yourself** for a Fresh encounter with God. Pray and ask God to speak to you. (Psalm 37:7)

2.   **Read** the Scripture of the Day and prepare to hear a **Fresh Word** from God. (II Timothy 3:16-17)

3.   **Respond** with the *"Mind of Christ"* by writing down what God has said to you through the Scripture and the devotional thoughts. (Jeremiah 33:3)

4.   **Reflect** as you *"Experience God"* by listening to His Voice and writing down your prayers and thoughts. (John 16:23)

5.   **Rely** on Jesus to help you live out these truths. (Luke 11:28) Ask, *"Lord, what do you want me to do today?"*   (God's to-do list.)

(Pray for strength as you put on the Full Armor of God.)

Face to Face With God

Saul hated Jesus and all those who believed in His way. To Saul, Jesus was a heretic and a cancer in Judaism. Thus, all followers of His doctrine must be killed or imprisoned. Saul was headed to Damascus to eradicate believers there when something happened. He met Jesus. A brilliant light appeared, brighter than the noon sun. Was this the Shekinah glory of God? It was God pursuing man. Jesus asked Saul, "Why do you persecute Me?" Jesus was identifying Himself with His church (His Body). Whatever is done to a Christian is done as unto Christ. Jesus is also giving Saul the message that HE IS ALIVE. When Saul asks Jesus to identify Himself in confirmation, Jesus replies "I am Jesus you are persecuting." Jesus was sending Saul another message. He was saying in effect, "Jesus - the self-existent, eternal I AM. JESUS IS JEHOVAH."

Imagine Saul's thoughts. Everything that he believed was wrong. He had just seen the King of Glory. This was necessary in order to authenticate him later as an apostle. (I Cor. 9:1). However, this vision scorched his eyeballs. Metaphorically, once we've seen Jesus we'll never be the same again! Saul obeys the Lord and goes to Damascus. He then did what we all should do when in trials or spiritual warfare - he fasted and prayed.

Reflect a moment on your own conversion experience. Remember how you discovered who Jesus really is and how you "saw" Him the first time. In your pilgrimage, believer, never forget the way back to your "Damascus Road."

My Quiet Time Journal

1.   Ready yourself for a Fresh encounter with God. Pray and ask God to speak to you. (Psalm 37:7)

2.   Read the Scripture of the Day and prepare to hear a **Fresh Word** from God. (II Timothy 3:16-17)

3.   Respond with the *"Mind of Christ"* by writing down what God has said to you through the Scripture and the devotional thoughts. (Jeremiah 33:3)

4.   Reflect as you *"Experience God"* by listening to His Voice and writing down your prayers and thoughts. (John 16:23)

5.   Rely on Jesus to help you live out these truths. (Luke 11:28) Ask, *"Lord, what do you want me to do today?"*   (God's to-do list.)

(Pray for strength as you put on the Full Armor of God.)

When God Calls

Who was Ananias? His faithfulness is recorded in the eternal Word of God. God uses the obscure, the weak, and the humble. We must offer our lives to be used by Him however he wishes and then respond in obedience. When God calls someone to a specific task, He is already working in other areas to accomplish His will. Notice that God gave Saul his vision of Ananias before God spoke to Ananias (v. 12). God knew Ananias' devotion to God and his fellow men (Acts 22:12). What does God know about you?

Ananias acts like we do when God tells us to do something. We either question God's wisdom or feel like we have to remind Him of some fact. Imagine thinking that we know more than the Designer of the Universe! But, God is long-suffering. God tells Ananias, "Go!" Ananias does not deserve an explanation but God gives him one anyway.

All of us are chosen vessels like Saul to bear Jesus' name to the whole world. If we live godly and publicly as Jesus' disciples, we shall suffer persecution. Perhaps, God mentioned Saul's future sufferings to Ananias because of the suffering of the church at the hands of Saul (v 13). (For a list of Paul's sufferings, confer to II Cor. 11:23-28. Also, according to legend, Paul was beheaded by Nero).

When Saul received the Holy Spirit by the laying on of Ananias' hands, scales fell from his eyes and he could see. Spiritually, is this not what happened at our conversion? We were blind to God but now we see. Praise God! Saul became an excited convert. He immediately witnessed about Jesus the Christ.

My Quiet Time Journal

1. **Ready yourself** for a Fresh encounter with God. Pray and ask God to speak to you. (Psalm 37:7)

2. **Read** the Scripture of the Day and prepare to hear a **Fresh Word** from God. (II Timothy 3:16-17)

3. **Respond** with the *"Mind of Christ"* by writing down what God has said to you through the Scripture and the devotional thoughts. (Jeremiah 33:3)

4. **Reflect** as you *"Experience God"* by listening to His Voice and writing down your prayers and thoughts. (John 16:23)

5. **Rely** on Jesus to help you live out these truths. (Luke 11:28) Ask, *"Lord, what do you want me to do today?"* (God's to-do list.)

(Pray for strength as you put on the Full Armor of God.)

Week Six- Day Six

Acts 9:22-31

Growing

Between verses 21 and 22, we can probably insert Saul's excursion to Arabia where he receive revelations from God and, after which, his relationship to Jesus was growing. The Holy Spirit quickened Old Testament scripture to Saul's keen trained mind so that he could refute his old associates and prove that Jesus is the Messiah. (The whole Bible is about Jesus and God's plan of redemption for fallen man.) The Jews considered Saul a dangerous traitor and desired to kill him. Believers, may we be dangerous to the Kingdom of Satan by our testimony of Jesus Christ, our Lord!

The Jerusalem church distrusted Saul. If Barnabas ("Son of Encouragement") had not vouched for Saul's character, Saul would not have been accepted. Instead, Saul confronted the Grecian Jews (the group that had instigated Stephen's martyrdom). In the book of Acts, we see how the Holy Spirit empowers the witnesses of Jesus to speak "boldly."

Compare verse 31 with 8:1. This week, we have seen how God has taken something terrible and changed it into a blessing in accordance to His will. It was God's will that believers of the Lord Jesus Christ testify of Him beyond Jerusalem (Acts 1:8). Now, it's time to move from Judea and Samaria "unto the uttermost part of the earth."

My Quiet Time Journal

1.   Ready yourself for a Fresh encounter with God. Pray and ask God to speak to you. (Psalm 37:7

2.   Read the Scripture of the Day and prepare to hear a **Fresh Word** from God. (II Timothy 3:16-17)

3.   Respond with the *"Mind of Christ"* by writing down what God has said to you through the Scripture and the devotional thoughts. (Jeremiah 33:3)

4.   Reflect as you *"Experience God"* by listening to His Voice and writing down your prayers and thoughts. (John 16:23)

5.   Rely on Jesus to help you live out these truths. (Luke 11:28) Ask, *"Lord, what do you want me to do today?"*   (God's to-do list.)

(Pray for strength as you put on the Full Armor of God.)

Acts 9:32-43

Lives that Bear Witness

Peter did not sit at ease in Jerusalem. He was a traveling evangelist who went throughout the country. In Lydda, he healed a paralytic of eight years, Aeneas, in the name of Jesus Christ. Because of this miracle, many in Lydda and Sharon believed Peter's message and turned to Christ. In Scripture, miracles were performed to authenticate that a prophet or messenger was from God.

In Joppa, a disciple got sick and died. Dorcas was "full of good works" and was always helping the poor. Her death was a great loss to those in Joppa. Why was Dorcas so important? Because she was always SERVING OTHERS in the name of Jesus. Notice the great faith of the disciples of Joppa. They sent for Peter to come, believing that Jesus would raise up Dorcas through Peter! That's exactly what happened. Dorcas was resuscitated as a testimony to the awesome power and the unlimited love of Almighty God. Because of this miracle, many in Joppa turned to Jesus by believing the Gospel message. Those who were already believers increased in faith.

Peter lodged many days with a tanner in Joppa. Apparently, Peter was not concerned about being ceremonially unclean: (Lev. 11:35-40). Step by step, God was moving Peter from legalism to liberty that is in Christ. Interestingly, it was in Joppa that Jonah fled from God's commission to preach to the Gentiles. It is at Joppa that God tells Peter to use the Keys of the Kingdom of heaven for the Gentiles (Acts 10).

My Quiet Time Journal

1. **Ready yourself** for a Fresh encounter with God. Pray and ask God to speak to you. (Psalm 37:7)

2. **Read** the Scripture of the Day and prepare to hear a **Fresh Word** from God. (II Timothy 3:16-17)

3. **Respond** with the *"Mind of Christ"* by writing down what God has said to you through the Scripture and the devotional thoughts. (Jeremiah 33:3)

4. **Reflect** as you *"Experience God"* by listening to His Voice and writing down your prayers and thoughts. (John 16:23)

5. **Rely** on Jesus to help you live out these truths. (Luke 11:28) Ask, *"Lord, what do you want me to do today?"* (God's to-do list.)

(Pray for strength as you put on the Full Armor of God.)

Week Seven - Day One

Acts 10:1-8

When an Angel of the Lord Speaks

Cornelius was one of the most important men who ever lived. Yet most people today could not identify him. Why was he so important? Because God chose him to be the first Gentile convert, and through his conversion the door of salvation was opened to the Gentile world. The Apostles understood the commission Christ had given them. But until Cornelius was converted, they only preached to Jews and Samaritans. The Apostles had not realized a Gentile could be brought into the Body of Christ.

Cornelius had been attracted to the God of the Jews and had begun to pray and give money. He was doing everything he knew to come into a personal relationship with God, but nothing worked. Yet God observed Cornelius and prepared the way for his salvation.

As we read what the angel said, we are struck with a question. Why didn't the angel speak to him of repentance toward God and faith in our Lord Jesus Christ? Why didn't the angel share the Gospel with him? Because God doesn't use angels to share the Gospel. As we saw in Acts 2, He uses people like you and me. In order to reach the next generation, it is up to us!

Is that true in your city? Are there more people ready to listen to the Gospel than there are people ready to give it? Is that true in your neighborhood? Do you identify with that problem? In Jesus' day also, the harvest was plentiful, but the laborers were few (Matthew 9:37). Even today, in spite of thousands of training clinics, workshops, and conferences, there is still a dire shortage of spiritually qualified laborers.

When the Angel of the Lord speaks, respond!

My Quiet Time Journal

1. **Ready yourself** for a Fresh encounter with God. Pray and ask God to speak to you. (Psalm 37:7)

2. **Read** the Scripture of the Day and prepare to hear a **Fresh Word** from God. (II Timothy 3:16-17)

3. **Respond** with the *"Mind of Christ"* by writing down what God has said to you through the Scripture and the devotional thoughts. (Jeremiah 33:3)

4. **Reflect** as you *"Experience God"* by listening to His Voice and writing down your prayers and thoughts. (John 16:23)

5. **Rely** on Jesus to help you live out these truths. (Luke 11:28) Ask, *"Lord, what do you want me to do today?"* (God's to-do list.)

(Pray for strength as you put on the Full Armor of God.)

Acts 10:9-22

Do Not Hesitate to Go

The World is waiting to hear the Gospel. God is at work all around us preparing hearts to see and hear the Gospel. God wants to use every "born again" Believer to share what God has done and is doing in their lives. He is preparing your life to use you! God prepared a man to witness to this Roman centurion, Cornelius. Peter was on a rooftop praying. Under normal circumstances, Peter might not have responded to the invitation of the men from Caesarea. But Peter was in prayer, the Lord prepared his heart through an unusual vision. So, guided by the Holy Spirit, Peter agreed to go.

There are a number of important lessons for us in this event. God wanted his man to launch out on this mission in complete assurance of faith, without misgivings. So He took the time to settle the matter in Peter's heart. Unless a person is absolutely convinced he is in the will of God, his life and witness bear little fruit and have little power.

Paul's constant declaration that he was an Apostle by the will of God was more than just a means of assuring his readers he was ministering in the name of Christ, with His blessing. It contains one of the secrets of Paul's ministry. He was living in God's will, and he knew it. God used the fact to inflame Paul's spirit with courage and zeal.

If we want to be used by God, we must first make sure how God wants to use us, and then press on in that direction with great dedication. This was the attitude with which the Lord wanted Peter to go forth. And with this attitude, we also must go forth!

"Do not hesitate to go with them, for I have sent them." (Acts 10:20).

My Quiet Time Journal

1. Ready yourself for a Fresh encounter with God. Pray and ask God to speak to you. (Psalm 37:7)

2. Read the Scripture of the Day and prepare to hear a **Fresh Word** from God. (II Timothy 3:16-17)

3. Respond with the *"Mind of Christ"* by writing down what God has said to you through the Scripture and the devotional thoughts. (Jeremiah 33:3)

4. Reflect as you *"Experience God"* by listening to His Voice and writing down your prayers and thoughts. (John 16:23)

5. Rely on Jesus to help you live out these truths. (Luke 11:28) Ask, *"Lord, what do you want me to do today?"* (God's to-do list.)

(Pray for strength as you put on the Full Armor of God.)

Acts 10:23

Our Mission

In Acts 10:23, Peter took some men with him when he went. Did he take them to carry the luggage? Did they go to run errands or to help with the travel arrangements? They may have done some of those things, but that certainly wasn't the main reason why Peter took them. This was Peter's "generation next".

Peter's mission in life was making disciples. Jesus made that abundantly clear in His Commission to the Apostles. Peter had walked and talked with Jesus for three years. He knew the powerful effect that training by association had on his own life. It was all so simple—so unassuming.

There were no highly structured seminars, classes, institutes, or workshops like those we're so familiar with. There was no teacher equipped with a power point presentation, retractable pointer, charts, white board, or outlines of systematic theology. Of course I don't disapprove of such things. Whatever can be used to train men and women in the Christian life should be used. We are all called to disciple.

But we are foolish or blind if we omit the basic training method Jesus used. He primarily trained His men by association on the job. To forget that, to do everything but that, and implement a training program that neglects the principle of connection is not a complete program. Peter understood this principle of training, so he took some men along with him. He followed the pattern Jesus created when training the Twelve Disciples. They were discipled.

Our mission is to follow the pattern Jesus created and train disciples to spread the Word of God, that all might know Him. "The next day Peter started out with them and some of the brothers...went along." (Acts 10:23).

My Quiet Time Journal

1.   Ready yourself for a Fresh encounter with God. Pray and ask God to speak to you. (Psalm 37:7)

2.   Read the Scripture of the Day and prepare to hear a **Fresh Word** from God. (II Timothy 3:16-17)

3.   Respond with the *"Mind of Christ"* by writing down what God has said to you through the Scripture and the devotional thoughts. (Jeremiah 33:3)

4.   Reflect as you *"Experience God"* by listening to His Voice and writing down your prayers and thoughts. (John 16:23)

5.   Rely on Jesus to help you live out these truths. (Luke 11:28) Ask, *"Lord, what do you want me to do today?"*   (God's to-do list.)

(Pray for strength as you put on the Full Armor of God.)

Lord of All
(One at a time)

In opening the door of faith to the Gentiles, God selected one man and started with him. This was consistent with God's plan down through the ages. Through His Son He would offer redemption to the world. This strategy is so profound in its simplicity that we miss it! Many times we overlook the potential of one life! Peter quickly explained to Cornelius how unusual it was for him to make such a visit to a Gentile's home. "You are well aware," he said, "that it is against our law for a Jew to associate with a Gentile or visit him. But God has shown me that I should not call any man impure or unclean." (Acts 10:28).

The Jews regarded the Gentiles as unclean. They referred to Gentiles as dogs. In his prayers, a Jew thanked God daily that he was not a Gentile. To the Jewish mind the Gentile was less than nothing, filthy, and unclean. A Jew was forbidden by law to enter a Gentile's home. But Peter told Cornelius, "God has shown me some things, He led me here, and I am at your service." (Acts 10:29) Cornelius gave his account of the story and concluded by telling Peter his entire household had gathered to hear Peter's message from God.

Peter's first remark was a mind blower to the men traveling with him. Peter said, "Of a truth I perceive that God is no respecter of persons: But in every nation he that feareth Him, and worketh righteousness, is accepted with Him." (Acts 10:34-35) The Jews had always assumed that God was a respecter of persons. They believed God had chosen them, and rejected everyone else. They had missed God's great purpose for them and forgotten the clear teaching of Scripture. "For the Lord your God is God of gods and Lord of lords, the great God, mighty and awesome, who shows no partiality...? Deut. 10:17). He is not just Lord, but "Lord of All."

My Quiet Time Journal

1. **Ready yourself** for a Fresh encounter with God. Pray and ask God to speak to you. (Psalm 37:7)

2. **Read** the Scripture of the Day and prepare to hear a **Fresh Word** from God. (II Timothy 3:16-17)

3. **Respond** with the **"Mind of Christ"** by writing down what God has said to you through the Scripture and the devotional thoughts. (Jeremiah 33:3)

4. **Reflect** as you **"Experience God"** by listening to His Voice and writing down your prayers and thoughts. (John 16:23)

5. **Rely** on Jesus to help you live out these truths. (Luke 11:28) Ask, **"Lord, what do you want me to do today?"**   (God's to-do list.)

(Pray for strength as you put on the Full Armor of God.)

Acts 10:39-48

The Lordship of Christ

Peter's experiences with Jesus, and his submission to the Lordship of Christ, prepared him to be the man who unlocked the Kingdom of God to the Gentiles during his visit with Cornelius. When he spoke in Cornelius' home, after making a few more introductory comments, Peter proclaimed the Gospel. The Gospel is the power of God unto salvation." (Romans 1:16).

After sharing the Gospel, Peter went back to the foundation of our faith. He said God had "commanded us to preach to the people and to testify that He (Jesus) is the one appointed by God to judge the living and the dead. " (see also Ephesians 2:8-20). And he goes on to say that God has appointed us to "preach". We are called and appointed by God to share the Gospel story. God wants us to be clear and share "our Gospel stories" of how God has changed our lives. As a result God's Holy Spirit was poured out on everyone who was hearing. Why? Because the Holy Spirit that lives in us comes out of us as we speak His Word and His Truth. When you tell the Gospel from God's Word it is God's Spirit that speaks through you. Will you let Him use you to share His Truths.

God can do the impossible. When your world falls apart and there seems to be no way out, God can do what is impossible for man to do. Share God's Gospel, share how that Gospel has become "your story" of Truth that saves.

My Quiet Time Journal

1. **Ready yourself** for a Fresh encounter with God. Pray and ask God to speak to you. (Psalm 37:7)

2. **Read** the Scripture of the Day and prepare to hear a **Fresh Word** from God. (II Timothy 3:16-17)

3. **Respond** with the *"Mind of Christ"* by writing down what God has said to you through the Scripture and the devotional thoughts. (Jeremiah 33:3)

4. **Reflect** as you *"Experience God"* by listening to His Voice and writing down your prayers and thoughts. (John 16:23)

5. **Rely** on Jesus to help you live out these truths. (Luke 11:28) Ask, *"Lord, what do you want me to do today?"* (God's to-do list.)

(Pray for strength as you put on the Full Armor of God.)

God Makes No Junk!

Have you ever heard the phrase "God makes no junk"? It means that everyone is created in the image of God. Everyone is important to God. And it is so true. But, the Jewish nation was prejudice. To the Jewish way of thinking, Peter committed three unpardonable sins. He had entered a Gentile's household, eaten with the family, and to make matters worse, had baptized a group of Gentiles into the church. The Jewish Christians felt insulted because those Gentiles had not been circumcised before they were baptized. For the Jews, such behavior was an insult to God, a departure from Scriptures and their national history.

To help them understand what he had done, Peter "explained everything to them precisely as it had happened." (Acts 11:4) He began with his vision in Joppa and explained how God had led him to Caeserea where he met Cornelius.

When the Jews heard that the Holy Spirit had been given to the Gentiles, in the same way he had been given to them on the day of Pentecost, they were convinced. It had been a long, uphill battle to bring the Gentiles into the Kingdom. But once again the Lord had won. His Kingdom of priests were finally on the move. It had taken some time, but progress is often slow.

"The voice spoke from heaven a second time, 'Do not call anything impure that God has made clean." (Acts 11:9).

We cannot be prejudice. God wants us to share the Gospel story with everyone. God wants to save everyone. (John 3:16)

My Quiet Time Journal

1. **Ready yourself** for a Fresh encounter with God. Pray and ask God to speak to you. (Psalm 37:7)

2. **Read** the Scripture of the Day and prepare to hear a **Fresh Word** from God. (II Timothy 3:16-17)

3. **Respond** with the *"Mind of Christ"* by writing down what God has said to you through the Scripture and the devotional thoughts. (Jeremiah 33:3)

4. **Reflect** as you *"Experience God"* by listening to His Voice and writing down your prayers and thoughts. (John 16:23)

5. **Rely** on Jesus to help you live out these truths. (Luke 11:28) Ask, *"Lord, what do you want me to do today?"* (God's to-do list.)

(Pray for strength as you put on the Full Armor of God.

Acts 11:19-30

Good News

So it was with God and His people. At long last, He finally had them on track, heading in the right direction. They understood that Gentiles, as well as Jews, should be welcomed into the Kingdom. Apart from a few minor setbacks, the church became a lively witness to the Gentile world.

On the day of Pentecost, people from many nations listened to the message. People from Cyrene were there, and it is quite likely that some of them were among those who began to share the Good News with the Gentiles. God blessed their ministry. Remember, these were not the leaders of the church. They were laborers, trained by the Apostles. They were not the Apostles, but their lifestyle bore a striking resemblance to that of the Apostles. We reproduce spiritually after our own kind. That is what happened in the instance recorded in Acts 11. They proclaimed new life in the Lord Jesus Christ. The results? "A great number believed and turned to the Lord." (Acts 11:21) Sounds familiar doesn't it? The Apostles had done their job. They had trained these laborers effectively.

Consider the city to which the Lord led this band of men. Antioch was known as the Third City of the Roman Empire. Its worship of Ashtaroth was accompanied with immoral indulgence and unbelievable indecency. Yet multitudes of its people accepted Christ. It became the birthplace of the name "Christian" and the center of organized efforts to Christianize the world.

Why would God send this missionary band to such a place? Surely there were some cities which could have provided a gentler training ground for those fledgling laborers! But why not Antioch? Who needs to hear the Gospel more? Also, if these disciples succeeded in such a setting, it would be a clear demonstration to everyone that the Gospel could succeed anywhere!

My Quiet Time Journal

1.   Ready yourself for a Fresh encounter with God. Pray and ask God to speak to you. (Psalm 37:7)

2.   Read the Scripture of the Day and prepare to hear a **Fresh Word** from God. (II Timothy 3:16-17)

3.   Respond with the *"Mind of Christ"* by writing down what God has said to you through the Scripture and the devotional thoughts. (Jeremiah 33:3)

4.   Reflect as you *"Experience God"* by listening to His Voice and writing down your prayers and thoughts. (John 16:23)

5.   Rely on Jesus to help you live out these truths. (Luke 11:28) Ask, *"Lord, what do you want me to do today?"*   (God's to-do list.)

(Pray for strength as you put on the Full Armor of God.)

Acts 12:1-16

The Great Escape!

Herod was trying to please the Jews again, but God had different plans. He apparently was teaching two parties trust and reliance upon Him. The Disciples were at home praying fervently for Peter and his deliverance. Peter had failed earlier in his faith. Perhaps the disciples remembered Peter's lack of faith when they offered up their prayers. Were their prayers effective? Absolutely! Where do we find Peter at this time? He was guarded by sixteen men and chained between two of them. He had to pass at least two other sets of guards and an iron gate to get to freedom. He had been in jail a short time, and the next day was his trial date. What was his posture? He was ASLEEP! He was on his way to losing his head in court within twenty-four hours, but he was asleep, knowing and trusting that God was in control. He was resting "in the LORD". On the day of Pentecost, the Holy Spirit had given divine assurance, and Peter was learning and experiencing true faith and trust. The Disciples were fervently praying. They were exhibiting their faith, through prayer, that God would take care of Peter. Perhaps they did not know what to expect. In any case they were fervently praying with faith and trust themselves. This type of prayer is "on your knees, grit your teeth, stay at it, offer the request up with sweat" kind of prayer. Jesus was fervent in prayer in the garden. Moses was fervent in prayer for the Israelites when they had built the golden calf, and God wanted to wipe them out. Undoubtedly the Disciples had maintained a close relationship with the Father. In this time of trial they offered their request up to God for Peter's safety. "The effectual fervent prayer of a righteous man avails much." (James 5:16, KJV) God delivered. Let's all pray!

My Quiet Time Journal

1.   Ready yourself for a Fresh encounter with God. Pray and ask God to speak to you. (Psalm 37:7)

2.   Read the Scripture of the Day and prepare to hear a **Fresh Word** from God. (II Timothy 3:16-17)

3.   Respond with the *"Mind of Christ"* by writing down what God has said to you through the Scripture and the devotional thoughts. (Jeremiah 33:3)

4.   Reflect as you *"Experience God"* by listening to His Voice and writing down your prayers and thoughts. (John 16:23)

5.   Rely on Jesus to help you live out these truths. (Luke 11:28) Ask, *"Lord, what do you want me to do today?"*   (God's to-do list.)

(Pray for strength as you put on the Full Armor of God.)

Acts 12:7-11

Signed, Unsealed, And Delivered

Peter was dead asleep. Suddenly, he was struck on the side. He snapped awake and thought he was having a vision or dreaming. The very dark prison was now fully lit. He heard some commands. He obeyed. The sense of wonder appeared to override any fears or concerns Peter had because he rose and the chains fall off. The dream continues . . . or is it a dream? Our chains can fall off. The Christian's weapons "have divine power to demolish strongholds . . . and every pretension that sets itself up against the knowledge of God . . ." (II Corinthians 10:4-5 NIV). We must gird ourselves up and shoe our feet with the Gospel of Peace, put on the belt of Truth just as Peter commanded, and be ready to stand in the evil day and obey as we are commanded. Peter did. He followed this shining person past two sets of sleeping guards clomping along in his wooden sandals. Having just dropped heavy chains that clanked as they fell, Peter still thought he was dreaming, until he got outside after the door swung open by itself. Then the shining one disappeared. When I trust God I can suddenly find myself delivered. My heart is not to be trusted. The things that I would do, I do not do. The things I do not want to do are the very things I do! Oh, wretched man that I am, who can save me from this body of sin? (Romans 7:15-24) I confess, am sorry, request forgiveness, am cleansed, and request empowerment through the blood of Jesus to not do it again. I now request His presence *daily* so that when the temptation comes, He *is* there and will control me if I am willing to let Him. Jesus is *my personal* deliverer from myself. Peter was delivered. I am also. Now let's share this truth with others.

My Quiet Time Journal

1. **Ready yourself** for a Fresh encounter with God. Pray and ask God to speak to you. (Psalm 37:7)

2. **Read** the Scripture of the Day and prepare to hear a **Fresh Word** from God. (II Timothy 3:16-17)

3. **Respond** with the *"Mind of Christ"* by writing down what God has said to you through the Scripture and the devotional thoughts. (Jeremiah 33:3)

4. **Reflect** as you *"Experience God"* by listening to His Voice and writing down your prayers and thoughts. (John 16:23)

5. **Rely** on Jesus to help you live out these truths. (Luke 11:28) Ask, *"Lord, what do you want me to do today?"* (God's to-do list.)

(Pray for strength as you put on the Full Armor of God.)

Acts 12:12-17

Astonishment!

Prayer works. I am usually in awe and sometimes astonished when answers to prayers come about. It's those times I hear God say, "Well, you asked Me, didn't you?" Often I sense His smile. He is pleased to answer the requests of His children. He knows what I am thinking, but He wants to talk with me and hear me talk with Him. Without that communication, can there be an intimate relationship? God wants us to pray and hear Him speak.

God knew the disciples very well. Daily affairs seemed very grim. Just their very existence in Jerusalem looked bleak. Rhoda responded, as most of us probably would, with astonishment. So astonished, in fact, that she forgot to open the door. Remember that a lot of continual prayer had been offered for Peter, probably for days, and when deliverance came, theirs was a natural response: astonishment. Rhoda was as persistent as Peter.

Open the door. Dare to see answered prayer in the flesh. What would this do for you? Look around and see God at work. My faith is strengthened every time I hear a testimony of answered prayer or someone recognizing God working in their life. The Disciples were the same. Peter encouraged them that prayer works and, for their safety and his, left for another place. We all want to hear this.

If opportunity presents itself for you to share answered prayer, don't deny the people around you the blessing of hearing about God working. Faith comes by hearing . . . (Romans 10:17).

My Quiet Time Journal

1.   Ready yourself for a Fresh encounter with God. Pray and ask God to speak to you. (Psalm 37:7)

2.   Read the Scripture of the Day and prepare to hear a **Fresh Word** from God. (II Timothy 3:16-17)

3.   Respond with the *"Mind of Christ"* by writing down what God has said to you through the Scripture and the devotional thoughts. (Jeremiah 33:3)

4.   Reflect as you *"Experience God"* by listening to His Voice and writing down your prayers and thoughts. (John 16:23)

5.   Rely on Jesus to help you live out these truths. (Luke 11:28) Ask, *"Lord, what do you want me to do today?"*   (God's to-do list.)

(Pray for strength as you put on the Full Armor of God.)

Week Eight - Day Four

Acts 12:18-23

Pride or Humility

Where do I get my sense of self worth? How can I be built up in my life? Herod had slowly acquired material wealth, and positions. He derived his whole sense of self-worth from his status. He knew of God, the Jewish laws and ways, and even of Jesus, the Messiah, but rejected these by his own choosing, his own way.

God often uses the world's ways and "vessels of wrath" to point out sinful attitudes or situations to His children. When the world is our focus it seems to teach us lessons the hard way. Herod just soaked up the praise as his own, never acknowledging God as Provider and Lord. He paid a huge price, his life. Where is your focus?

"...I am gentle and humble in heart . . .," Jesus said. (Matthew 11:29) God is an awesome God who is worthy of all my praise and worship. He has provided all things for my need. Can I be anything but humble at His provision? The question is incorrectly stated: In what do I get my sense of self-worth? In giving up the "what" for "Whom," I find out who I really am. I don't want the situation to get "wormy" for me. I must take the experiences of this life and look at them through the lenses of faith in Jesus as my source. I must look at the ways of the world as lessons of what not to do and follow the LORD at what I need to do. And then I need to share these truths with the next generation of believers. I must discuss discipleship!

My Quiet Time Journal

1.   Ready yourself for a Fresh encounter with God. Pray and ask God to speak to you. (Psalm 37:7)

2.   Read the Scripture of the Day and prepare to hear a **Fresh Word** from God. (II Timothy 3:16-17)

3.   Respond with the *"Mind of Christ"* by writing down what God has said to you through the Scripture and the devotional thoughts. (Jeremiah 33:3)

4.   Reflect as you *"Experience God"* by listening to His Voice and writing down your prayers and thoughts. (John 16:23)

5.   Rely on Jesus to help you live out these truths. (Luke 11:28) Ask, *"Lord, what do you want me to do today?"*   (God's to-do list.)

(Pray for strength as you put on the Full Armor of God.)

The Last Straw

Being set apart for Jesus' work is special. When we become new Christians, Jesus accepts us as we are. We begin a new pilgrimage that prepares us for a particular service in His Kingdom. Being a new Christian doesn't hinder our ability to serve. Our growth is God's plan so that we can be more useful when He calls us to serve. Saul and Barnabas were set apart and sent to Cyprus from Antioch. The Holy Spirit did the selecting; the brethren agreed by laying hands on them, and they were sent out with their blessings. Saul and Barnabas reflected many traits of a laborer (versus a disciple): hunger for the Word, conviction of Scripture reading, prayer, fellowship, witnessing, ministry skills, personal holiness, concern for others and their potential, a servant's heart, cooperation, and availability. God developed these areas in preparation for the area of service they were assigned. We are all developed or are being developed in areas of service for God. Barnabas and Saul (now called Paul) ran into spiritual warfare. In witnessing to Paulus, the proconsul, Satan intervened with a sorcerer, Bar-Jesus. Paul confronted him face to face and rebuked him such that the consequence was blindness. The miracle convinced Paulus that Jesus is the Christ, and he believed. This was the proverbial "last straw" for Paulus. As we share the blessings Christ has poured into our lives, it can become the "last straw" for those who've been drawn to Christ but are hovering on the outskirts of belief. When you feel the urge to share, God is usually not working solely in your life. Share the blessing. In doing so you bless others, and usually plant a seed, water, fertilize, shine on, or otherwise encourage another person. Your obedience may result in heavenly treasure for you and bring another soul to know Jesus.

My Quiet Time Journal

1.   Ready yourself for a Fresh encounter with God. Pray and ask God to speak to you. (Psalm 37:7)

2.   Read the Scripture of the Day and prepare to hear a **Fresh Word** from God. (II Timothy 3:16-17)

3.   Respond with the *"Mind of Christ"* by writing down what God has said to you through the Scripture and the devotional thoughts. (Jeremiah 33:3)

4.   Reflect as you *"Experience God"* by listening to His Voice and writing down your prayers and thoughts. (John 16:23)

5.   Rely on Jesus to help you live out these truths. (Luke 11:28) Ask, *"Lord, what do you want me to do today?"*   (God's to-do list.)

(Pray for strength as you put on the Full Armor of God.)

Paul's Persuasion About Jesus

This is one example of Paul reasoning concerning Jesus in the synagogues with the Jews and God-believing Gentiles. Using the Scriptures, Paul reveals Jesus throughout the Holy Scriptures from the Egyptian bondage of the Israelites through David to John the Baptist and the history of the cross and its meaning. Paul states the facts and puts everything concerning Jesus out in front of his listeners very plainly, even to the point of saying, "Don't be left out!" Notice how pointed Paul's speech was. He cut through religious differences, political issues, intellectualism, and economic problems, not mentioning them once. He concentrated fully on Jesus. Look in verse 17 at the word "chose." God chose fathers, he chose leaders, he chose people to do His work. God has chosen you and me to become His children, if we believe Jesus is the Christ. Paul's example of a historical persuasion to the point of Jesus and His work on the cross is a model of concise reasoning; a "scarlet thread" that runs through history and the Bible. That "scarlet thread" is the atoning work of Jesus which continues to run through our history, present, and future. God is calling individuals to intimate relationship with Him, conforming them into the image of His Son. The result? The Great Commission is being fulfilled. Make disciples! From the testimony of the youngest Christian to one who has been in Christ all their life, the scarlet thread continues to run. Don't quench the Spirit which prompts you to move out and speak for Jesus. He grants the words to say and things to do if we are willing to "be" or remain in Him. What happens when I don't see the good in a circumstance? Trust God. He sees the whole puzzle of my life and how best to live it. He knows how the pieces fit. Also, the circumstances that I encounter are filtered through God's system of approval as part of His role as Shepherd. He has my best interest at heart.

My Quiet Time Journal

1.   Ready yourself for a Fresh encounter with God. Pray and ask God to speak to you. (Psalm 37:7)

2.   Read the Scripture of the Day and prepare to hear a **Fresh Word** from God. (II Timothy 3:16-17)

3.   Respond with the *"Mind of Christ"* by writing down what God has said to you through the Scripture and the devotional thoughts. (Jeremiah 33:3)

4.   Reflect as you *"Experience God"* by listening to His Voice and writing down your prayers and thoughts. (John 16:23)

5.   Rely on Jesus to help you live out these truths. (Luke 11:28) Ask, *"Lord, what do you want me to do today?"*   (God's to-do list.)

(Pray for strength as you put on the Full Armor of God.)

Acts 13:44-52

The Jews Get Dusted

Jealousy is a terrible master. The Jews were filled with it when they saw the response of the city to Paul's words. It only took seven days for his words to become the talk of the town; "Almost the whole city gathered to hear the word of the Lord." (verse 44) Jealousy built a resistance to God's Word in the Jews like a stone wall. They refused to listen any further to anything Paul was saying. Not only this, but the Jews stirred up the city officials to have then thrown out of the region. Paul withstood them, "we had to speak the Word of God to you first." And later (verse 51) Paul and Barnabas "dusted" them off, " . . . shook the dust from their feet in protest against them." (verse 51) The Gentiles were another story. They, " . . . were glad and honored the Word of the Lord." (verse 48) The result was awesome. The Word of the Lord spread through the whole region. In spite of Paul and Barnabas' ejection, God's Word was firmly entrenched and prospered among the believers. *Am I like the Jews, Lord? I read the Word and see something that "confuses" me, because it is contrary to my ways and thinking. I wish to be your vessel of clay, Lord, to be molded as You see fit. Open my ears and heart to yield to Your perfect teaching.* The Creator knows what is best for His creation, especially His child. The word for this week has been deliverance. *Father, deliver me from myself that I might nail my old self to Your cross daily, that my life might be pleasing to you, for the furtherance of You Kingdom, and that You might be glorified through me. In Your precious Son's name, Jesus, I pray. Amen.*

My Quiet Time Journal

1.   Ready yourself for a Fresh encounter with God. Pray and ask God to speak to you. (Psalm 37:7)

2.   Read the Scripture of the Day and prepare to hear a **Fresh Word** from God. (II Timothy 3:16-17)

3.   Respond with the *"Mind of Christ"* by writing down what God has said to you through the Scripture and the devotional thoughts. (Jeremiah 33:3)

4.   Reflect as you *"Experience God"* by listening to His Voice and writing down your prayers and thoughts. (John 16:23)

5.   Rely on Jesus to help you live out these truths. (Luke 11:28) Ask, *"Lord, what do you want me to do today?"*   (God's to-do list.)

(Pray for strength as you put on the Full Armor of God.)

OH BE... CAREFUL LITTLE TONGUE WHAT YOU SAY!

Do you remember singing that little song when you were a child? I do. You have read in the Bible several times that the tongue is a powerful part of the human body. Paul and Barnabas discovered this. In 14:2 "Jews who refused to believe stirred up the Gentiles and poisoned their minds against the brothers." Paul and Barnabas had been sharing the truth and many had accepted Christ but some of the Jews didn't like it, so they began to talk. We've all been there. Something doesn't go the way we think it should or the way it's been done in the past and we "mention" it to someone. Look at what happened when the Jews began to talk. The minds of the people were "poisoned." by someone else's personal opinion. Oh, be careful little tongue what you say. We all must be careful.

Let's look at something else. In verse 3, Paul and Barnabas spent extra time with these very people who were against them. The Bible says the Lord "confirmed" their message by allowing them to do miracles. The word confirmed implies that action took place before that. I think back to Abraham. The sacrificial ram did not appear until after Isaac was on the altar and the knife was raised. God confirmed Abraham's belief that a sacrifice would be provided only after Abraham took action. The world will treat you with hostility. Stand firm and God will prove Himself faithful. The world will give you opportunities to voice your personal opinion. Let's just share Jesus instead.

My Quiet Time Journal

1.   Ready yourself for a Fresh encounter with God. Pray and ask God to speak to you. (Psalm 37:7)

2.   Read the Scripture of the Day and prepare to hear a **Fresh Word** from God. (II Timothy 3:16-17)

3.   Respond with the ***"Mind of Christ"*** by writing down what God has said to you through the Scripture and the devotional thoughts. (Jeremiah 33:3)

4.   Reflect as you ***"Experience God"*** by listening to His Voice and writing down your prayers and thoughts. (John 16:23)

5.   Rely on Jesus to help you live out these truths. (Luke 11:28) Ask, ***"Lord, what do you want me to do today?"***   (God's to-do list.)

(Pray for strength as you put on the Full Armor of God.)

Acts 14:8-18

LET'S ALL SPEAK THE SAME LANGUAGE

In his book, Disciples in Action, Leroy Eims give an
interesting illustration. He can be sitting in a room filled
with Dutchmen, Chinese, or Indonesian who are all
speaking English but if something humorous or exciting is
mentioned, each man will revert back to his native tongue.
This is all well and good, provided you are not the only
native-tongued, English speaking person in the room. If
you are, you could feel pretty lonely in a room full of
people. Do you ever think that people in churches tend to
speak "Churchese" and that people who haven't been in
church before or have been in church for a short time don't
understand. Put yourself in their place. You come to a
worship service at your Church looking for help and
someone to love you. But when you get there you aren't
dressed like everyone else, you don't understand what is
going on, and no one stops to try to speak your language.
You could feel pretty lonely in that large crowd, couldn't
you? Paul and Barnabas ran into this problem in verse 11.
The people began to shout in the Lycaonian language. Did
this persuade Paul and Barnabas to stop preaching. No.
They got in the street where the people were and did the
best they could to speak their language and continue to
share with them the truth. Are we as a church willing to
speak the language of the lost and hurting? Paul and
Barnabas did what it took to communicate. The ran into
the street and ripped their clothes. That probably got the
people's attention! The point here is, they had something
important to give away and would do whatever it took to
communicate, or speak their language. Are we willing to
do the same? Are we willing to disciple anyone?

My Quiet Time Journal

1.   Ready yourself for a Fresh encounter with God. Pray and ask God to speak to you. (Psalm 37:7)

2.   Read the Scripture of the Day and prepare to hear a **Fresh Word** from God. (II Timothy 3:16-17)

3.   Respond with the *"Mind of Christ"* by writing down what God has said to you through the Scripture and the devotional thoughts. (Jeremiah 33:3)

4.   Reflect as you *"Experience God"* by listening to His Voice and writing down your prayers and thoughts. (John 16:23)

5.   Rely on Jesus to help you live out these truths. (Luke 11:28) Ask, *"Lord, what do you want me to do today?"*   (God's to-do list.)

(Pray for strength as you put on the Full Armor of God.)

Acts 14:19-20

Press On!

Have you ever felt the whole world is against you? We've all been there at one time or the other. Things at work are tough, family life is not all we thought it would be, and to make matters worse, you found a new gray hair while gazing into the mirror this morning. Man, it's gonna be a great day! Sound familiar? Let's look at a biblical example of one who didn't let the thought of another day at the office get him down. Paul has been preaching the gospel to the people and they have been responding. It's taken quite an effort to win them over but he can see triumph just over the horizon. Then the opposition shows up. In verse 19 some Jews come from Antioch and Iconium and persuaded the crowd to believe them instead of Paul. What happens next is not a pretty picture. They stone him. What is Paul's response? Does he yell and scream for mercy? Does he plead his case until the mob relents? It does not appear that he did. He probably could have gotten out of this situation by denying Christ and walking away but he chose to press on, even when the world was against him. The people took him outside the city and left him for dead. This leads us to believe he must have been in pretty bad shape. Thank goodness for friends! The disciples gathered around and told him how bad he looked and that he had better get out of there. Not!! They gathered around him, encouraged him, loved on him and because of this, he was able to get up and go right back into the city that had just tossed him out on his can. You've heard it said "No man is an Island." It is important that we as brothers and sisters in the Lord be there for one another. Who can you help to get up and shake the dust off and press on? Believe me, they're out there if you're really looking. We all need to step up and help others.

My Quiet Time Journal

1. **Ready yourself** for a Fresh encounter with God. Pray and ask God to speak to you. (Psalm 37:7)

2. **Read** the Scripture of the Day and prepare to hear a **Fresh Word** from God. (II Timothy 3:16-17)

3. **Respond** with the *"Mind of Christ"* by writing down what God has said to you through the Scripture and the devotional thoughts. (Jeremiah 33:3)

4. **Reflect** as you *"Experience God"* by listening to His Voice and writing down your prayers and thoughts. (John 16:23)

5. **Rely** on Jesus to help you live out these truths. (Luke 11:28) Ask, *"Lord, what do you want me to do today?"* (God's to-do list.)

(Pray for strength as you put on the Full Armor of God.)

Week Nine – Day Four

Acts 14:21-26

The Characteristics of a Disciple

We have already been seeing that a Disciple is a "learner" and a Disciple maker is one that teaches disciples. It is our job to do whatever it takes to help a disciple grow and know how to live the Christian life. That is because we are all called to be a disciple and to go and make disciples. And our job is clearly spelled out in the Great Commission found in Jesus' words in Matthew 28:18-20 when he commands us to "go and make disciples." Well what are the characteristics of a disciple? In other words, how can go and "make" someone something when I don't even know what it is I am supposed to be doing?

Here we find a clear definition of what a disciple maker is to do.   In chapter 14 beginning in verse 21 through verse 23, we see three key things Paul and Barnabas did to make disciples. They are returning to Antioch to check up on how things are going. When they arrived they *strengthened* the disciples (v. 22), they *encouraged them to remain true* to the faith saying "We must go through many hardships to enter the kingdom of God" (v. 22). Just think, Paul, the man who was just stoned and left for dead, only calls his stoning experience a "hardship." Had I been Paul, I probably could have made a little more out of it than that! Rather than looking for sympathy for what he had been through, he is here encouraging others who may or may not have been through even half of what he had endured. So we are called to help these "learners" learn by training (strengthening), encouragement, and setting the example of dedication (remaining true).

My Quiet Time Journal

1.   Ready yourself for a Fresh encounter with God. Pray and ask God to speak to you. (Psalm 37:7)

2.   Read the Scripture of the Day and prepare to hear a **Fresh Word** from God. (II Timothy 3:16-17)

3.   Respond with the ***"Mind of Christ"*** by writing down what God has said to you through the Scripture and the devotional thoughts. (Jeremiah 33:3)

4.   Reflect as you ***"Experience God"*** by listening to His Voice and writing down your prayers and thoughts. (John 16:23)

5.   Rely on Jesus to help you live out these truths. (Luke 11:28) Ask, ***"Lord, what do you want me to do today?"***   (God's to-do list.)

(Pray for strength as you put on the Full Armor of God.)

Acts 15:1-21

Our Rules or God's Rules?

Things never change. Have you ever heard that statement? I know I have many times in my life. Here's another. The more things change, the more they stay the same. Have you ever wondered if that is really true? Let's prove it is by using Acts 15 as an example. A discussion is brewing between some Jewish leaders and Paul and Barnabas. The topic happens to be circumcision, but it could have been most any topic. Why? Because the discussion wasn't really about the issue at hand but about tradition and opinion. Paul and Barnabas were teaching the new covenant of Jesus Christ. Under this covenant, the one we still live under, one only need confess his sins, ask forgiveness, believe in Jesus, and ask Jesus to save him and it's a done deal. The Jewish leaders wanted to add to these requirements. So, they take the issue up with the apostles and elders. Peter points out in v. 8-9 that God, who knows the heart, gave the Holy Sprit for all with no distinctions between us and them. Then James steps in, in v. 13. He speaks the heart of the message in v. 19 saying "we should not make it difficult for the Gentiles who are turning to God." In other words saying, let's meet them where they are. If you make it too difficult, they will not want to believe. How does this apply today? Simple. Just as the Jewish leaders wanted everyone else to do things their way, we want everyone to do things our way, even if it's just our own personal opinion. We expect everyone who visits our church to act like we act and do like we do. There are our ideas, not God's. God only requires that they believe. In an instant gratification society, people will not jump over man made hurdles to come to know Christ. Rather than expecting everything to be done one way or the other, celebrate the diversity God has brought to His church. As disciples mature in Christ they will learn to obey God's Word specifically.

My Quiet Time Journal

1. **Ready yourself** for a Fresh encounter with God. Pray and ask God to speak to you. (Psalm 37:7)

2. **Read** the Scripture of the Day and prepare to hear a **Fresh Word** from God. (II Timothy 3:16-17)

3. **Respond** with the *"Mind of Christ"* by writing down what God has said to you through the Scripture and the devotional thoughts. (Jeremiah 33:3)

4. **Reflect** as you *"Experience God"* by listening to His Voice and writing down your prayers and thoughts. (John 16:23)

5. **Rely** on Jesus to help you live out these truths. (Luke 11:28) Ask, *"Lord, what do you want me to do today?"* (God's to-do list.)

(Pray for strength as you put on the Full Armor of God.)

Week Nine – Day Six

Acts 15:22-35

When it absolutely, positively has to get there

Do you remember that slogan that one of the overnight delivery companies used several year ago? "When it absolutely, positively has to be there overnight." What they were trying to say to you is you can trust them. They've been in the business for a while and they know what they are doing. Don't we like to know that the people we are following know what they are doing and are in charge of the situation? This is exactly what was going on in this passage of scripture.

Word needed to be sent to the church at Antioch. They needed to be encouraged and kept on the right path. Some people had come to the church on behalf of the leaders back in Jerusalem but if fact they had not been sent by the leadership. They were acting on their own volition and had apparently spread confusion in the church. The leaders in Jerusalem wanted to set it right and it had to be done now. When they went looking for someone to send to Antioch, they didn't send just anyone. They sent Judas and Silas with Paul and Barnabas. These were men who had "been in the business for a while." They had risked their life for the gospel. In other words, the truth of the gospel was too important to entrust its delivery to just anyone. They needed someone they could trust and someone they knew would deliver the message. They were committed and they were dependable. They had set the example.

Has anything changed today? The church is still in need of dependable leadership to help carry the message. People who have been through difficulties and come out the other with faith still in tact. Can your church depend on you? Are you one that will stand firm for the gospel of Jesus Christ? Can you share these truths with the next generation?

Are you a Judas or Silas, or a Paul or a Barnabas? When it absolutely, positively has to get done, can God count on you?

My Quiet Time Journal

1. **Ready yourself** for a Fresh encounter with God. Pray and ask God to speak to you. (Psalm 37:7)

2. **Read** the Scripture of the Day and prepare to hear a **Fresh Word** from God. (II Timothy 3:16-17)

3. **Respond** with the *"Mind of Christ"* by writing down what God has said to you through the Scripture and the devotional thoughts. (Jeremiah 33:3)

4. **Reflect** as you *"Experience God"* by listening to His Voice and writing down your prayers and thoughts. (John 16:23)

5. **Rely** on Jesus to help you live out these truths. (Luke 11:28) Ask, *"Lord, what do you want me to do today?"* (God's to-do list.)

(Pray for strength as you put on the Full Armor of God.)

Week Nine – Day Seven

Acts 15:36-41

Backtracking

Paul was constantly pushing ahead. He is the key to the letters we have in our Bible today. He affected the New Testament Church more than anyone except Jesus himself. You could say he was a driven man.   Before he was converted to Christ, he was driven to persecute Christians. He brought this same drive to spreading the gospel. God knew this which is probably why he was chosen. But in all of his desire to move ahead to new ground and evangelize new believers, look at v. 36 of chapter 15. He said to Barnabas, "let's go back and see how they are doing." He realized that you can't always plow straight ahead with no regard as to where you have been. Sometimes you need to go back and encourage. In v. 41 after Paul and Barnabas have parted ways, he goes throughout the region "strengthening" or encouraging the churches.   Often in our daily lives we only have eyes and energies for what lies ahead. What's next? Where are we going now? We must realize we don't all progress at the same speed and when this happens, someone will be left behind. Back in high school days when I ran laps with the football team, I was rarely if ever at the front of the pack. I was slower and it was difficult to keep up. It always meant so much when one of the faster ones at the front of the pack would drop back and encourage those of us who were by nature slower. It always inspired me to press on. We have that same opportunity as our church grows. Those in the spiritual forefront need to drop back and be an encourager sometimes. Our coach used to say that the real leaders were not the ones who stayed in the front, but those who dropped back to help others. Do you need to backtrack today and check on someone who is struggling?

My Quiet Time Journal

1.   Ready yourself for a Fresh encounter with God. Pray and ask God to speak to you. (Psalm 37:7)

2.   Read the Scripture of the Day and prepare to hear a **Fresh Word** from God. (II Timothy 3:16-17)

3.   Respond with the *"Mind of Christ"* by writing down what God has said to you through the Scripture and the devotional thoughts. (Jeremiah 33:3)

4.   Reflect as you *"Experience God"* by listening to His Voice and writing down your prayers and thoughts. (John 16:23)

5.   Rely on Jesus to help you live out these truths. (Luke 11:28) Ask, *"Lord, what do you want me to do today?"*   (God's to-do list.)

(Pray for strength as you put on the Full Armor of God.)

Acts 16:1-5

Training Syllabus

Paul recruits Timothy and invites him to join the team. Timothy was a disciple with a good reputation among the believers. Timothy also had a submissive heart. He followed Paul's instructions and wisdom. He had servant hands. He helped in ministry throughout Asia, and also in Macedonia when the time was right. (Acts 19:22) And finally Paul and Timothy were sensitive to the leading of the Holy Spirit. The decisions reached by the Jerusalem Council in Acts 15 was obviously Spirit-directed, and met with acceptance as Paul's team conveyed their decisions to the Churches. Thus the churches grew in faith and in numbers: a balance of Encouragement and Evangelism. Paul was establishing a training syllabus as he was recruiting laborers for the harvest. The harvest *is* truly plentiful, but the laborers are really few. (Matthew 9:37). We need more disciples. We need to reach the next generation. We need to pour our lives into faithful men and women who will be able to train others also (2 Timothy 2:2)

Are you ready to join God's team? To go God's way with a heart that is submissive to leadership? To have a heart that is willing to serve, and a life that is sensitive to the Holy Spirit? The evidence is a witness within itself.

God is calling you! The training syllabus is easy, the load is light. Yoke up with Jesus. Be a disciple maker.

My Quiet Time Journal

1.   Ready yourself for a Fresh encounter with God. Pray and ask God to speak to you. (Psalm 37:7)

2.   Read the Scripture of the Day and prepare to hear a **Fresh Word** from God. (II Timothy 3:16-17)

3.   Respond with the *"Mind of Christ"* by writing down what God has said to you through the Scripture and the devotional thoughts. (Jeremiah 33:3)

4.   Reflect as you *"Experience God"* by listening to His Voice and writing down your prayers and thoughts. (John 16:23)

5.   Rely on Jesus to help you live out these truths. (Luke 11:28) Ask, *"Lord, what do you want me to do today?"*   (God's to-do list.)

(Pray for strength as you put on the Full Armor of God.)

Week Ten - Day Two

Acts 16:6-15

Spiritual Control Shown

As Paul and his companions continued their journey, it is clear that the Holy Spirit was very much in control. He was leading at every "fork" in the road (the best is yet to come.) Jesus' promise of the Holy Spirit's guidance was being fulfilled exactly. But we see both the Holy Spirit and the Spirit of Jesus here. (Acts 16:6,7) Were these different? In personage, no! In manifestation, yes! The Holy Spirit was that voice working within the believer; whereas, the Spirit of Jesus was the Holy Spirit working through a believer. The same Spirit in different functions.

Then, an event occurred that changed the course of history! Paul learned that the Lord wanted him to go to Macedonia. (Acts 16:9-10). Luke writes; "*We* got ready at once...concluding that God had called *us.*" (Acts 16:10) Had God called Luke? Not specifically, but Luke considered himself a part of the team, and their leader was Paul. When God spoke to Paul, it was if God spoke to them all! This is what our church family is all about! As God speaks to us, He is speaking to us all! And in the next verses from Troas and following, the team continued in God's will together.

Unity! That's what teamwork is all about anyway! Allowing God to use us together to follow His Spirit as He directs all for the Glory of God and the Churches Good!

My Quiet Time Journal

1.   Ready yourself for a Fresh encounter with God. Pray and ask God to speak to you. (Psalm 37:7)

2.   Read the Scripture of the Day and prepare to hear a **Fresh Word** from God. (II Timothy 3:16-17)

3.   Respond with the *"Mind of Christ"* by writing down what God has said to you through the Scripture and the devotional thoughts. (Jeremiah 33:3)

4.   Reflect as you *"Experience God"* by listening to His Voice and writing down your prayers and thoughts. (John 16:23)

5.   Rely on Jesus to help you live out these truths. (Luke 11:28) Ask, *"Lord, what do you want me to do today?"*   (God's to-do list.)

(Pray for strength as you put on the Full Armor of God.)

Acts 16:16-40

Lessons

Now, of course, since God had called the team to Macedonia surely He would prepare the way with roses and sunshine. Well, maybe the thorns of the roses and the heat of the sunshine at least. But God knew what He was doing. Remember Isaiah 55:8-9; "For My thoughts are not your thoughts, neither are your ways, My ways declares the Lord. As the heavens are higher than the earth, so are My ways higher than your ways and My thoughts than your thoughts." Lydia had opened her heart to the Lord (Acts 16:14,15), the demon came out of the girl, and Paul and Silas were whipped and thrown into prison. But why? For several reasons: 1) To provide an opportunity for theses (including the Jailer) to be saved. 2) To encourage the believers in Lystra. 3) Most likely, as a great teacher, Paul used what happened to him to teach a great lesson. The first European Church was established on a basis of courage and dignity in the midst of wild and unlawful tumult. If Paul could make the magistrates think, maybe they would learn a lesson also.

What about you? What lessons do you seek to learn when you are faced with situations and circumstances that seem to be thorny? Do you look for the roses? I guess it's time!

Our World is looking for leaders and teachers that will allow discipleship to be lived out as well as spoken out. When we share our Gospel Stories we must be able to use the good, the bad, and the ugly to all be working together for the good and for God's Glory. These are the discipleship lessons.

My Quiet Time Journal

1. Ready yourself for a Fresh encounter with God.   Pray and ask God to speak to you. (Psalm 37:7)

2.   Read the Scripture of the Day and prepare to hear a **Fresh Word** from God. (II Timothy 3:16-17)

3.   Respond with the *"Mind of Christ"* by writing down what God has said to you through the Scripture and the devotional thoughts. (Jeremiah 33:3)

4.   Reflect as you *"Experience God"* by listening to His Voice and writing down your prayers and thoughts. (John 16:23)

5.   Rely on Jesus to help you live out these truths. (Luke 11:28) Ask, *"Lord, what do you want me to do today?"*   (God's to-do list.)

(Pray for strength as you put on the Full Armor of God.)

Acts 17:1-15

Keep Focused

Paul's journeys as a missionary continue as he traveled to Thessalonica. As was his custom, Paul entered the synagogue (Jewish church) and discussed with the men and women using the Old Testament (the new had not been written yet) why Jesus was the Christ, their Messiah, that they had been looking for. Mary believed and the movement continued to grow. But, as with any growth, and change, there were problems. Some of the Jews were jealous. They did not like the changes so they spread rumors and tried to cause problems.

So Paul and Silas moved away to Berea, and again shared the message of the Messiah (Jesus Christ) with the Jews there. The message was accepted eagerly and they examined the Scriptures to see the Truth. Problems still arose, but many Jews believed. Verse one of our text today says they passed through Amphipolis and Apollonia to come to Thessalonica. Whey did they pass through? Didn't people there need the Gospel too? Sure they did, but as we see in the rest of the verses, Paul and Silas were "purpose driven." God had given them a specific call, and they had to follow it! As a believer it is important to keep focused on the call on your life.

My Quiet Time Journal

1.   Ready yourself for a Fresh encounter with God. Pray and ask God to speak to you. (Psalm 37:7)

2.   Read the Scripture of the Day and prepare to hear a **Fresh Word** from God. (II Timothy 3:16-17)

3.   Respond with the *"Mind of Christ"* by writing down what God has said to you through the Scripture and the devotional thoughts. (Jeremiah 33:3)

4.   Reflect as you *"Experience God"* by listening to His Voice and writing down your prayers and thoughts. (John 16:23)

5.   Rely on Jesus to help you live out these truths. (Luke 11:28) Ask, *"Lord, what do you want me to do today?"*   (God's to-do list.)

(Pray for strength as you put on the Full Armor of God.)

Acts 17:16-34

Relevant

Paul entered Athens and saw the need of the city. It was a city filled with idolatry. He needed a discipleship plan but it was not going to be the old regular method.

The people there showed a genuine interest because Paul was relevant to their situation and circumstance. Paul met the Athenians "where they were" in their lives. As a result, they listened and questioned. This was true discipleship.

Any time one witnesses to someone who needs Christ, it is essential that they get to know them and that the message is relevant to their needs. We must meet these individuals where they are, find out who their "gods" are and what their "gods" look like. Their "gods" could be anything from shopping to television! But instead of condemning and criticizing their "gods," introduce them to Jesus and let the Holy Spirit do His work in them. John 16:8 says, "When He (the Holy Spirit) comes, He will convict the world of guilt in regard to sin." The Holy Spirit disciples through us to the next generation.

We no longer have to condemn or criticize. Simply introduce them to Jesus, and let the *Holy Spirit* convict them of their need. Make sure they understand in their own language and God will do the rest.

Be relevant so Jesus can bring redemption! Be authentic so the Holy Spirit can get their attention. Trust in God's Word to teach absolute Truth.

My Quiet Time Journal

1.   Ready yourself for a Fresh encounter with God. Pray and ask God to speak to you. (Psalm 37:7)

2.   Read the Scripture of the Day and prepare to hear a **Fresh Word** from God. (II Timothy 3:16-17)

3.   Respond with the *"Mind of Christ"* by writing down what God has said to you through the Scripture and the devotional thoughts. (Jeremiah 33:3)

4.   Reflect as you *"Experience God"* by listening to His Voice and writing down your prayers and thoughts. (John 16:23)

5.   Rely on Jesus to help you live out these truths. (Luke 11:28) Ask, *"Lord, what do you want me to do today?"*   (God's to-do list.)

(Pray for strength as you put on the Full Armor of God.)

Multiplication

In Acts 18 we find the Apostle Paul in Corinth. It's a location controlled by the trade routes between the Aegean and Adriatic seas. Greeks, Romans, and Middle Easterners meet in Corinth to do their business. The Apostle Paul knew that establishing a gospel witness there would spread the message far and wide. Paul went into action immediately after arriving in Corinth. He found a promising couple and began pouring his life into them. Discipleship was modeled in the discussions. He was eager to share with them the lessons he had learned about following Christ. We have seen this pattern time and time again. Paul knew his job but he also knew his limitations. He was just one man. If he could multiply his co-laborers, he would multiply his effectiveness. So Paul heard God speak, saw his value there, and stayed 18 months, and taught them the Word of God.

We, too, must learn the value of multiplication. God is calling each one of us to give away our faith. Just think: if each one disciples one in our fellowship alone, God *doubles* our church body! God can multiply our church by two easily if we will just listen, obey, and follow His direction. Do you need to be a part of this multiplication? Without a doubt! Rededicate yourself today so you can reproduce for the Kingdom's sake! We need to be disciplers!

My Quiet Time Journal

1.   Ready yourself for a Fresh encounter with God. Pray and ask God to speak to you. (Psalm 37:7)

2.   Read the Scripture of the Day and prepare to hear a **Fresh Word** from God. (II Timothy 3:16-17)

3.   Respond with the ***"Mind of Christ"*** by writing down what God has said to you through the Scripture and the devotional thoughts. (Jeremiah 33:3)

4.   Reflect as you ***"Experience God"*** by listening to His Voice and writing down your prayers and thoughts. (John 16:23)

5.   Rely on Jesus to help you live out these truths. (Luke 11:28) Ask, ***"Lord, what do you want me to do today?"***   (God's to-do list.)

(Pray for strength as you put on the Full Armor of God.)

Acts 18:18-28

Humble Boldness

After Paul had stayed in Corinth for over a year and a half, he took Priscilla and Aquilla on to Ephesus where he left them to minister. He then returned to Antioch. He spent some time in Cenchrea and Antioch, then set out again and traveled around to encourage the disciples.

Now we meet Apollos, a fervent eloquent man who had a thorough knowledge of the Word of God, and taught about Jesus accurately. Rarely do we meet someone as gifted and talented as Apollos who is still willing to learn and be taught. Apollos was eager to learn. He wanted to still be discipled. When he went to Achaia, he was a tremendous help. He encouraged the new believers, who needed his "humble boldness." This is the only way to describe Apollos. He was a humble servant filled with the Holy Spirit, a true man of God who was full of wisdom and knowledge, yet open to grow and serve. He was modeling discipleship also in his lifestyle.

We all need to follow this example. Humble and eager to learn, yet ready to give an account when needed. Peter said it clearly, "But in your hearts set apart Christ as Lord, always be prepared to give an answer...but do this with gentleness and respect." (1 Peter 3:15) That is *humble boldness!* Do you have it?

My Quiet Time Journal

1.   Ready yourself for a Fresh encounter with God. Pray and ask God to speak to you. (Psalm 37:7)

2.   Read the Scripture of the Day and prepare to hear a **Fresh Word** from God. (II Timothy 3:16-17)

3.   Respond with the **"Mind of Christ"** by writing down what God has said to you through the Scripture and the devotional thoughts. (Jeremiah 33:3)

4.   Reflect as you **"Experience God"** by listening to His Voice and writing down your prayers and thoughts. (John 16:23)

5.   Rely on Jesus to help you live out these truths. (Luke 11:28) Ask, **"Lord, what do you want me to do today?"**   (God's to-do list.)

(Pray for strength as you put on the Full Armor of God.)

A Little Knowledge is a Dangerous Thing

Paul arrived at Ephesus on his third missionary trip, having avoided the trade routes by taking the back roads. This was his third visit, and he wanted to renew friendships and encourage the church.   Upon his arrival he met twelve disciples that Apollos had led to Jesus. In their conversation Paul apparently sensed that something was wrong; there seemed to be an absence of the Holy Spirit in their lives. They had been baptized, but their understanding of baptism was that it signified repentance - John, the Baptist's baptism. Paul led them to understand that the Lord they professed would baptize them with the Holy Spirit. Professing this new Truth, they were baptized and received the Holy Spirit.   Jesus said that not everyone who called him Lord would enter the Kingdom of Heaven. (Matthew 7:21-23) If this is true, who *can* enter the Kingdom? If Jesus promises to send the Holy Spirit (John 16:7-15), why is it that some church members seem to live in two worlds - the world of the Kingdom on Sunday and world of the flesh during the rest of the week?   The answer is here. They have repented and been baptized, that want to do what is right in their "heads" but they have not given their hearts and lives to Jesus. The Holy Spirit has not taken up residence in their lives. They say, "Lord, Lord," but he does not know them. They are living with a false hope. Jesus will say, "I never knew you." (Matthew 7:23)   These disciples were then baptized, not re-baptized. Their first baptism was not of Jesus. Their second was real. How about your profession? Those whose baptisms are real are those who do the will of the Father. (Matthew 7)   The world is looking for truth. Jesus **is** Truth. Unless the world sees the Holy Spirit in our lives, they will not know Truth. Did your baptism *"take*?" Is God's will your will, or do you have two lives? The Lord will not accept your hypocrisy.   Know the joy of becoming a child of the King, a follower of the Lamb. Know the peace that surpasses anything that the world can give. (John 14:27). Give your heart and life to Jesus, not just your head.

My Quiet Time Journal

1.   Ready yourself for a Fresh encounter with God. Pray and ask God to speak to you. (Psalm 37:7)

2.   Read the Scripture of the Day and prepare to hear a **Fresh Word** from God. (II Timothy 3:16-17)

3.   Respond with the **"Mind of Christ"** by writing down what God has said to you through the Scripture and the devotional thoughts. (Jeremiah 33:3)

4.   Reflect as you **"Experience God"** by listening to His Voice and writing down your prayers and thoughts. (John 16:23)

5.   Rely on Jesus to help you live out these truths. (Luke 11:28) Ask, **"Lord, what do you want me to do today?"**   (God's to-do list.)

(Pray for strength as you put on the Full Armor of God.)

Week Eleven - Day Two

Acts 19:8-10

Sticks and Stones

"Sticks and stones may break my bones, but words will never harm me." So goes a saying familiar to most of us. Paul faced a similar situation in Ephesus. As was his custom, he went into the synagogue to teach. He "spoke boldly" for three months, apparently with good success, but there were those who disputed with him and publicly opposed the Gospel. Rather than arguing with those who refused to acknowledge that Jesus is Lord, he moved to another location, the lecture hall of Tyrannus, centrally located in the city. There he taught the disciples from eleven in the morning until four in the afternoon. It appears that Tyrannus used the hall from early morning until just before lunch and after four until the evening hours. Apparently the people of Ephesus avoided the hot hours of the day by taking a long lunch and an afternoon nap. Taking advantage of the opportunity that existed was a habit of Paul, and he spoke there for two years. All the people not only of Ephesus, but the whole province, heard the Gospel message! (Acts 19:10) It's so easy to compromise or give up when we face opposition. We don't want to hurt anyone's "feelings" or accept rejection. Rather than doing that, we just stop. Paul was successful in preaching the Gospel because he would not stop! People began to listen out of respect for his persistence. If he was so sure of himself there must be some truth to his words! How do we react when some "friend" tells us we are crazy when we talk about Jesus? What do we do when the world around us treats us with disrespect, maybe even laughs at our silly "faith?" Do we become silent? Are we afraid? Are we ashamed of the Gospel of Jesus Christ? How wonderful it would be to hear that *everyone* in the whole country heard about Jesus because of our testimony. Our world will be changed when we allow Jesus to speak his Truth through us. The devil has no power over the Word of God. It is only our fear and shame that holds us back, and this is of the devil. You can do **all** things through Christ who strengthens you, just as Paul did. (Phil. 4:13)

My Quiet Time Journal

1.   **Ready yourself** for a Fresh encounter with God. Pray and ask God to speak to you. (Psalm 37:7)

2.   **Read** the Scripture of the Day and prepare to hear a **Fresh Word** from God. (II Timothy 3:16-17)

3.   **Respond** with the *"Mind of Christ"* by writing down what God has said to you through the Scripture and the devotional thoughts. (Jeremiah 33:3)

4.   **Reflect** as you *"Experience God"* by listening to His Voice and writing down your prayers and thoughts. (John 16:23)

5.   **Rely** on Jesus to help you live out these truths. (Luke 11:28) Ask, *"Lord, what do you want me to do today?"*   (God's to-do list.)

(Pray for strength as you put on the Full Armor of God.)

Acts 19:11-20

The Power of the Gospel

Ephesus was the center of worship of Aremis, the goddess of fertility of the Ephesians and other gentile countries. It was also known for its magicians. Among practitioners of magic in ancient times, Jews enjoyed high respect. When Paul's ministry in Ephesus was marked by mighty works of divine power, particularly of healing and exorcism, it followed that adherents to magic would see an opportunity to take advantage of the situation.   Luke tells us that people were healed by means of pieces of material that had come in contact with Paul. (Acts 19:12) The materials used were those he used as sweat rags and aprons while engaged in tent making. Remember: Peter's shadow was thought to have a healing effect. (Acts 5:15) Non-believers saw the miracle of the new birth in those who believed in Jesus, and Satan clouded their minds, telling them it was magic.   The seven sons of a self-designated "Jewish Chief Priest" decided that the name of Jesus must hold magical qualities since Paul used it, and miracles occurred. But when they tried to use it, the evil spirits, through the man they inhabited, drove the seven sons away naked and wounded. They tried to use the name of Jesus, but, like an unfamiliar weapon wrongly handled, it exploded in their hands. (Acts 19:14-16) Isn't it amazing how the Lord uses *all things* to accomplish his will? The name of Jesus is so powerful that those who heard what had happened were filled with awe. Many who practiced the satanic powers of magic were convicted of the power of Jesus' name. They believed and confessed their sin, revealing their spells. According to magical theory, when a spell is revealed, it becomes ineffective. These magicians were giving up their livelihood for the sake of the Gospel. Burning their documents, valued at 50,000 day's wages, they defeated the powers of darkness, and the Gospel spread and triumphed!   The power of the name of Jesus, to those who believe, is eternal life. Nothing magical or otherwise can separate us from the love of God in Jesus, the Christ. (Romans 8:35-39).

My Quiet Time Journal

1. **Ready yourself** for a Fresh encounter with God. Pray and ask God to speak to you. (Psalm 37:7)

2. **Read** the Scripture of the Day and prepare to hear a **Fresh Word** from God. (II Timothy 3:16-17)

3. **Respond** with the *"Mind of Christ"* by writing down what God has said to you through the Scripture and the devotional thoughts. (Jeremiah 33:3)

4. **Reflect** as you *"Experience God"* by listening to His Voice and writing down your prayers and thoughts. (John 16:23)

5. **Rely** on Jesus to help you live out these truths. (Luke 11:28) Ask, *"Lord, what do you want me to do today?"* (God's to-do list.)

(Pray for strength as you put on the Full Armor of God.)

Time Moves On

Paul had been in Ephesus some two and a half years - longer than any other city he chose to use as a headquarters. It had been a fruitful and encouraging ministry. The churches in the Lycus Valley, Colossae, Hierapolis and Laodicea, were founded by disciples who had sat at Paul's feet to learn about Jesus. In fact, perhaps all of the seven churches of Asia addressed in the Revelation of John may have been founded about this time. Paul probably never visited any of them. (Colossians 2:1; 4:13) Now was the time to move on. It's always difficult to leave a situation when all is going so well. Paul, though, was focused on the Lord's plan for his life. He had no idea where that plan might lead him or what might befall him. He just knew that his life was the Lord's to direct.   It seems that Paul's master plan was to visit and establish churches in Spain, but his immediate goal was to visit Rome and meet the Christians already there. His plan was to travel through Macedonia and Achaia, visit Jerusalem with offerings for the suffering believers there, and then to Rome. Little did he know what was to become of him. Before Paul left Ephesus, though, an incident occurred that reveals the spread and strength of the Gospel. (A group of artists who made images of Artemis for the tourist trade saw their sales hurt by Paul's preaching that gods made by hands were no gods at all. Acts 7:48; 17:24) They attempted to start a riot in hopes of destroying the preaching of Christ forever! They incited the people who joined them in running to the 25,000 seat, open-air theatre of the city. There was complete disorder in the crowd! Luke records that the majority of the people had no idea why they were there. (Acts 19:32) In the end, order was restored, and the people returned to their business. The Lord called Paul to move on. It certainly was not easy. There were hundreds who became disciples through the preaching of Paul. They were like his own children. Still, he had to obey Christ.   Are you at ease in Zion? If the Lord speaks to you and tells you that there is a Macedonia in your life, would you listen and go? Or would you ignore the call in order to enjoy what you now have? Paul probably made it to Spain by way of Rome, although it was not the itinerary he would have planned. He would have liked to have done it his way, but was willing in the end to do it God's way.

My Quiet Time Journal

1.   Ready yourself for a Fresh encounter with God. Pray and ask God to speak to you. (Psalm 37:7)

2.   Read the Scripture of the Day and prepare to hear a **Fresh Word** from God. (II Timothy 3:16-17)

3.   Respond with the *"Mind of Christ"* by writing down what God has said to you through the Scripture and the devotional thoughts. (Jeremiah 33:3)

4.   Reflect as you *"Experience God"* by listening to His Voice and writing down your prayers and thoughts. (John 16:23)

5.   Rely on Jesus to help you live out these truths. (Luke 11:28) Ask, *"Lord, what do you want me to do today?"*   (God's to-do list.)

(Pray for strength as you put on the Full Armor of God.)

Don't Fall Asleep in Church!

Travel in Paul's day was not a matter of hours but of months. The description of his travels in Acts 20:1-3 probably lasted for a year or longer. The three months he spent in Greece, probably in Corinth, were the winter months of A.D. 57-58. Here he wrote the letter to the Romans, preparing them for his intended visit. He prepared the offering for the church in Jerusalem for shipment, but could not accompany it because of a threat on his life. Paul left Greece and retraced his steps back to Troas, in Mysia, where he stayed seven days. Apparently Luke had joined him at this time. Paul had a lot he wanted to tell the church in Troas. It seems that he knew he would never see them again, so he spoke until midnight. The meeting was in a second and third floor room, lit by candles and lamps. As you can imagine, the air was heated by the lamps and heavy with the moisture of perspiration. A young man named Eutychus was sitting in an open window, probably to catch a breath of fresh air, when he went to sleep and fell at least two stories to his apparent death. The people rushed to the body, where Paul covered the young man with his *own* body, much as Elijah and Elisha had done in I Kings 17:21 and II Kings 4:34ff. Paul announced that the boy lived! Returning to the upper room, Paul continued speaking. After midnight they "broke bread", and Paul continued speaking until daybreak. He then left. Luke tells us that the people took the young man home and were greatly comforted. (Acts 20:12). Sometimes it is difficult to sit in church, especially when the speaker goes on and on and on. Still, even after the distraction of the fall and the miracle, the people stayed until daybreak. Perhaps it was the urgency and conviction in the manner of Paul that kept them there.

When your Pastor speaks, after having spent much time in prayer and Bible study, he speaks with the conviction and urgency of "Thus says the Lord!" Our responsibility is to be fresh and rested to hear God's Word. Come prayerfully. Come expectantly, and the Holy Spirit will bless your heart!

My Quiet Time Journal

1.   Ready yourself for a Fresh encounter with God. Pray and ask God to speak to you. (Psalm 37:7)

2.   Read the Scripture of the Day and prepare to hear a **Fresh Word** from God. (II Timothy 3:16-17)

3.   Respond with the *"Mind of Christ"* by writing down what God has said to you through the Scripture and the devotional thoughts. (Jeremiah 33:3)

4.   Reflect as you *"Experience God"* by listening to His Voice and writing down your prayers and thoughts. (John 16:23)

5.   Rely on Jesus to help you live out these truths. (Luke 11:28) Ask, *"Lord, what do you want me to do today?"*   (God's to-do list.)

(Pray for strength as you put on the Full Armor of God.)

Finishing the Task

Paul probably wanted to stop again at Ephesus to see his dear children in the Lord, but his goal was to reach Jerusalem by Pentecost, the birthday of the church. To that end he bypassed Ephesus and traveled directly to Miletus where the ship was to remain for four days. Paul sent a message to the elders of the Ephesian church to meet him at Miletus. Ephesus was some thirty miles away, so it was probably the third day when they arrived. After Paul reminded the elders of his conduct among them, his humble and faithful service, his sorrows, the dangers that he faced due to Jewish hostility, his continuous proclamation of the Gospel to all people and his Christian instruction, he went on to tell them of his present plan to visit Jerusalem. It was not easy to go to Jerusalem. The Holy Spirit kept reminding him that prison and hardships faced him. (Acts 20:23) If this were so, why did he persist in going? The answer is found in verse 22. Paul was "compelled by the Spirit." He *had* to go! The Lord never promised us a rose garden in our life. He only promises to go with us wherever He sends us. Paul understood that truth. Having already suffered beating and imprisonment, he knew that "in all things God works for good." (Romans 8:28) Still, we wonder how he, knowing the warnings, could continue the journey. His explanation is found in Acts 20:24. Paul saw his life as meaningless unless he finished the task that the Lord Jesus had given him. In II Timothy 4:7, in preparation for his death, Paul has completed his task. How focused are you in your obedience to the voice of the Holy Spirit in your life? Can you say that your life is meaningless without Jesus? Are you ready to go wherever He sends you, even with the warning that you may face prison and hardship - even death? Show the world what Jesus means to you!

My Quiet Time Journal

1.   Ready yourself for a Fresh encounter with God. Pray and ask God to speak to you. (Psalm 37:7)

2.   Read the Scripture of the Day and prepare to hear a **Fresh Word** from God. (II Timothy 3:16-17)

3.   Respond with the *"Mind of Christ"* by writing down what God has said to you through the Scripture and the devotional thoughts. (Jeremiah 33:3)

4.   Reflect as you *"Experience God"* by listening to His Voice and writing down your prayers and thoughts. (John 16:23)

5.   Rely on Jesus to help you live out these truths. (Luke 11:28) Ask, *"Lord, what do you want me to do today?"*   (God's to-do list.)

(Pray for strength as you put on the Full Armor of God.)

A Farewell Warning

Paul told the church leaders that this meeting was a last farewell. They would never see him again. The shocking statement certainly stunned them! They could not say a word, but they listened intently to Paul's every word. If he got safely away from Jerusalem, the western Mediterranean was to be his field of action. (Romans 15:23ff) He had planted the Gospel seed, and it was their responsibility to water it. Like the trustworthy watchman in Ezekiel 33:1-6, Paul sounded the trumpet so that all of Asia had heard. If they refused to hear, their blood was on their heads. Paul was free of responsibility. The Holy Spirit had entrusted these elders with the charge of the people of God in Ephesus. They had to care for them as shepherds care for their flocks. Savage wolves would be stalking the flock to attack the weak ones in order to scatter them. It is possible that some of them might even be wolves in shepherd's clothing! They must be on continuous guard. (Acts 20:28-31)   Paul reminded them to follow his example. (Acts 20:32-35) He quoted Jesus saying, "It is more blessed to give than to receive." Although Paul would not be there to counsel and guide, God was ever with them, and so was the Word of God which they had received. Paul committed them to these truths.   Kneeling in prayer with them as they wept, Paul completed the parting. If there were such a thing, they probably sang "Blest be the Tie that Binds." The ship was about to sail from Miletus, and the Ephesian elders escorted Paul to the deck before returning home.

As brothers and sisters in Christ, we share both joy and sorrow. At the same time, we are called upon to care for one another. Satan is seeking for whom he would devour. (I Peter 5:8). Are you on guard? Are you ready to share?

The Lord has done great things among us, and He continues to work miracles here. Satan is watching every one of us, hoping to catch us in a weak moment. Be alert! Pray without ceasing! Walk every day in the Spirit, and the evil one cannot prevail!

My Quiet Time Journal

1.   Ready yourself for a Fresh encounter with God. Pray and ask God to speak to you. (Psalm 37:7)

2.   Read the Scripture of the Day and prepare to hear a **Fresh Word** from God. (II Timothy 3:16-17)

3.   Respond with the *"Mind of Christ"* by writing down what God has said to you through the Scripture and the devotional thoughts. (Jeremiah 33:3)

4.   Reflect as you *"Experience God"* by listening to His Voice and writing down your prayers and thoughts. (John 16:23)

5.   Rely on Jesus to help you live out these truths. (Luke 11:28) Ask, *"Lord, what do you want me to do today?"*   (God's to-do list.)

(Pray for strength as you put on the Full Armor of God.)

Week Twelve - Day One

Acts 21:1-14

Keep On Keeping On

The Apostle Paul was at the end of his third missionary journey. He had been proclaiming the Good News of Jesus Christ to the Gentiles (non-Jews). Paul had devoted a good part of this journey to taking up a love gift from the Gentiles for the Jews in Judea. This was a practical way that the Gentiles showed both their oneness and their thankfulness to the Jews for sharing the Gospel with them. (Romans 15:25-27).

In the churches there was a constant threat of division. The Jewish extremists (the Judaizers) wanted the Gentiles to live like Jews and to follow the laws of Moses. (Acts 15:1) Wherever Paul ministered these extremists tried to hinder his work and steal his converts. Paul hoped that his visit to Jerusalem with the offering would strengthen the fellowship between the Jews and Gentiles.

In spite of two warnings not to go up to Jerusalem and face the extremists (Acts 21:4,12), Paul continued to push toward Jerusalem. He boldly said that even if he were to be bound up and killed in the name of the Lord, he was ready! (Acts 21:13).

We could accuse Paul of compromise, or we could applaud him for his courage. Paul was willing to give even his life to see the offering delivered and the division reconciled between the Jews and Gentiles in Jerusalem.

Do you have the courage and perseverance to press on in your calling? What one thing do you need to do today that will keep you on the course of faith relating to God's call in your life? Is there a divisions or confrontational issue that you need to deal with and work through? Do the thing you fear, and the death of fear will be certain! If you're at the end of your rope, tie a knot and hang on.

My Quiet Time Journal

1.   Ready yourself for a Fresh encounter with God. Pray and ask God to speak to you. (Psalm 37:7)

2.   Read the Scripture of the Day and prepare to hear a **Fresh Word** from God. (II Timothy 3:16-17)

3.   Respond with the *"Mind of Christ"* by writing down what God has said to you through the Scripture and the devotional thoughts. (Jeremiah 33:3)

4.   Reflect as you *"Experience God"* by listening to His Voice and writing down your prayers and thoughts. (John 16:23)

5.   Rely on Jesus to help you live out these truths. (Luke 11:28) Ask, *"Lord, what do you want me to do today?"*   (God's to-do list.)

(Pray for strength as you put on the Full Armor of God.)

Acts 21:15-40

Relationship Precedes Rules

When Paul stepped into Jerusalem with the disciples, they were gladly received. The second day there, he greeted the leaders in the church at Jerusalem. One by one he related to them the things God had done in their ministry with the Gentiles. Are you detailed with others (one by one) with what God is doing through your life? Be reminded that God usually works in you before he works *through* you. So, what is God doing in you? Are you responding with obedience (constant glad surrender)? God is in the business of building character before conduct, belief before behavior, changing *you* before He changes others.

God loves ALL men with partiality, how about you?

After a short time Paul was noticed in the temple (where Jesus worshiped). The Jews stirred up trouble for Paul and accused him of breaking their traditions. (Acts 21:28) We must all be careful not to allow the traditions of men to override or supersede the Truth of God. Perhaps you need your comfort zone stirred up. Be alert that your *relationship* with Jesus precedes the *rules*. (John 14:15) Maybe you're easily agitated or quickly offended. Would you please lay down your pride, your rules, and your comfort zones, and simply develop a close, intimate, personal relationship with Jesus?! Love is at the core of the Gospel, not your rules or your prejudices. God loves *ALL* men without partiality; how about you?

Because of Paul's relationship with Jesus and the rules of the extremist Jews, the city was aroused and in an uproar. The Jews were ready to kill Paul, but first he had to stand trial.

My Quiet Time Journal

1.   Ready yourself for a Fresh encounter with God. Pray and ask God to speak to you. (Psalm 37:7)

2.   Read the Scripture of the Day and prepare to hear a **Fresh Word** from God. (II Timothy 3:16-17)

3.   Respond with the **"Mind of Christ"** by writing down what God has said to you through the Scripture and the devotional thoughts. (Jeremiah 33:3)

4.   Reflect as you **"Experience God"** by listening to His Voice and writing down your prayers and thoughts. (John 16:23)

5.   Rely on Jesus to help you live out these truths. (Luke 11:28) Ask, **"Lord, what do you want me to do today?"**   (God's to-do list.)

(Pray for strength as you put on the Full Armor of God.)

Acts 22:1-3

Evangelistic Bait: Love

After the big uproar in the city, Paul had the opportunity to defend himself before the mob. Paul piled up his Jewish credentials. (Acts 22:3) How could these Jews not respectfully listen to him? Note how Paul baited their attention with Jewish language (Hebrew) and his Jewish background (law, education, zeal). How much do we bait our audience before we share the Gospel? The most powerful way for you to prepare others to hear the Gospel is to show them first. Oh, for your life to be a life of Love. Love covers a multitude of sins. (I Peter 4:8) Bait your hook with Love, cast out into this harsh world, and expect a catch! Everyone is starved for consistent, unfailing Love.

God is the Source of all Love

God is Love. God is the Source of all Love. You cannot express consistent, unfailing Love without first experiencing it. How do you move Love in the head (knowing) to Love in the heart (feeling)? How do you truly internalized the Love of God? This is the solution for low self-image, guilt, shame, rejection, and pain. How do I internalize the Love of God?

The only way you can internalize anything in life is through practice: just do it! If you would just follow the Holy Spirit's small nudge to say, "I love you", or give a hug , or go the extra mile, or cry with someone, or (you fill in), then God will begin internalizing His Love in you. Surely, we allow our pain, rejection, shame, guilt, and many other emotional hindrances to dam up God's Love and keep it from flowing into our hearts for the ultimate experience.

My Quiet Time Journal

1.   Ready yourself for a Fresh encounter with God. Pray and ask God to speak to you. (Psalm 37:7)

2.   Read the Scripture of the Day and prepare to hear a **Fresh Word** from God. (II Timothy 3:16-17)

3.   Respond with the *"Mind of Christ"* by writing down what God has said to you through the Scripture and the devotional thoughts. (Jeremiah 33:3)

4.   Reflect as you *"Experience God"* by listening to His Voice and writing down your prayers and thoughts. (John 16:23)

5.   Rely on Jesus to help you live out these truths. (Luke 11:28) Ask, *"Lord, what do you want me to do today?"*   (God's to-do list.)

(Pray for strength as you put on the Full Armor of God.)

Week Twelve - Day Four

Acts 22:4-10

Who Are You Persecuting?

Paul had baited his audience in order for them to perk up and take note of his defense and testimony. He then shared the experience which he had with Jesus Christ. Paul had been zealous to kill Christians and to persecute the Way. But, as he was on the road to Damascus to persecute Christians, a phenomenal thing happened in his life! Jesus asked Paul, "Why are you persecuting Me?" (Acts 22:7) Notice, He didn't ask, "Why are you persecuting the Church or Christians?" You see, if a Christian is persecuted, whether by attitude, action, or word, then Jesus is hurt. Jesus is the Head of the Church. We are joined to **Him** as one body. If one body part hurts, the whole body hurts, even the head. (Ephesians 4:15-16; 1 Corinthians 12:25-27)

Many have stopped the hand of God and grieved the Holy Spirit in their life because of their words.

Who did you *judge* recently with your pharisaical attitude? Who did you *speak* about, speak against recently, with your malicious, gangrene, trashy, mouth? You judged; therefore, you spoke against Jesus your Savior who died for you. Will you be more careful not to persecute others? Many of you actually stop the hand of God and grieve the Holy Spirit in your life because of your words. (Ephesians 4:29-30).

Will you now commit yourself to speak ill of no man? With the Psalmist David, will you purpose (chose, decide) that your mouth will not transgress (sin)? (Psalm 17:3, 39:1).

Here is a daily word for you to confess:

"I will not speak contrary to God's Word."

Say this over and over. Write it down. Speak it.

My Quiet Time Journal

1.   Ready yourself for a Fresh encounter with God. Pray and ask God to speak to you. (Psalm 37:7)

2.   Read the Scripture of the Day and prepare to hear a **Fresh Word** from God. (II Timothy 3:16-17)

3.   Respond with the *"Mind of Christ"* by writing down what God has said to you through the Scripture and the devotional thoughts. (Jeremiah 33:3)

4.   Reflect as you *"Experience God"* by listening to His Voice and writing down your prayers and thoughts. (John 16:23)

5.   Rely on Jesus to help you live out these truths. (Luke 11:28) Ask, *"Lord, what do you want me to do today?"*   (God's to-do list.)

(Pray for strength as you put on the Full Armor of God.)

Acts 22:11-21

He's Speaking. Are You Listening?

Paul was led by the hand to Damascus because the bright light had blinded his eyes. Once there, Ananias prophesied over Paul regarding things to come. God spoke to Paul of what he should do at the moment of need. (Acts 22:18,21) Often, we argue and try to compromise with God. Apparently, we think our way is best! As many of you know, there are primarily four ways God speaks to His people. He speaks to us by the Holy Spirit through the Bible, prayer, people (church, and circumstances. If you need direction and guidance in an area of your life, you should pray.

First, get specific with God. Understand that prayer will purify your motives as to whether the thing you are praying about is godly. Second, listen to the Holy Spirit, Who will surely match your need with God's provision (His Word).

Open your eyes, open your ears, open your heart to God. He's Speaking!

God's Word has the answer and solution to your needs and questions. Are you willing to listen to God's Word and do it? Are you willing to seek counsel from godly people as well as listen to your circumstances?

After purifying your motives concerning a need through prayer (James 4:3), look with expectancy for an answer in God's Word, your circumstances, and godly counsel. God is always speaking. Are you always listening? Open your eyes, open your ears, and open your heart to God. He's speaking!

My Quiet Time Journal

1. **Ready yourself** for a Fresh encounter with God. Pray and ask God to speak to you. (Psalm 37:7)

2. **Read** the Scripture of the Day and prepare to hear a **Fresh Word** from God. (II Timothy 3:16-17)

3. **Respond** with the *"Mind of Christ"* by writing down what God has said to you through the Scripture and the devotional thoughts. (Jeremiah 33:3)

4. **Reflect** as you *"Experience God"* by listening to His Voice and writing down your prayers and thoughts. (John 16:23)

5. **Rely** on Jesus to help you live out these truths. (Luke 11:28) Ask, *"Lord, what do you want me to do today?"* (God's to-do list.)

(Pray for strength as you put on the Full Armor of God.)

Acts 22:22-23:10

Know Your Audience

As Paul shared what Jesus had done in his life, note how real this experience was to him. As you share what God has done in your life, share what you know with enthusiasm, details, and boldness. After Paul shared his testimony with the mob, they were ready to rip him apart! In their minds, there was no way God would lead a Jew to minister to the Gentiles. (Acts 22:21-22) What a racist statement! Be reminded that Jesus Christ came to break down the cultural and racial walls that separate us from "others." (Ephesians 2:11-16). God is not a respecter of persons, but He *is* a respecter of faith in people.

Do you really know the people you are around everyday?

After many accusations from the mob, Paul was taken before a council to be tried. Paul, a wise man, used his understanding of the different religious groups (Sadducees and Pharisees) to raise an issue concerning the resurrection. This moved the focus from Paul and created a discussion and division among the groups. An amateur knows what to say, but a professional knows his audience. Paul used his understanding of the audience to win favor with the Pharisees, in spite of their threats.

Do you really know the people that you are around everyday? As you begin to know their needs, ask God for a creative way to make His message relevant in their arena. Be careful and ready because God's heart is to save the lost, and He will give you "creative juice" to meet the needs around you. Ask and listen. God is ready. How about you?

My Quiet Time Journal

1. **Ready yourself** for a Fresh encounter with God. Pray and ask God to speak to you. (Psalm 37:7)

2. **Read** the Scripture of the Day and prepare to hear a **Fresh Word** from God. (II Timothy 3:16-17)

3. **Respond** with the *"Mind of Christ"* by writing down what God has said to you through the Scripture and the devotional thoughts. (Jeremiah 33:3)

4. **Reflect** as you *"Experience God"* by listening to His Voice and writing down your prayers and thoughts. (John 16:23)

5. **Rely** on Jesus to help you live out these truths. (Luke 11:28) Ask, *"Lord, what do you want me to do today?"* (God's to-do list.)

(Pray for strength as you put on the Full Armor of God.)

Acts 23:12-35

Confess What You Possess

As Paul continued to minister in interesting ways with the mob, he won favor and made enemies. Paul didn't really create conflict; however, it was his stand for God's will for his life and for what was right that created conflict. Standing for God's will and God's ways may bring conflict with others around you. Deuteronomy 28:7 says, "The Lord will cause your enemies who rise up against you to be defeated before you; they shall come out against you one way and shall flee before you seven ways." Walk and live in faithful obedience, and let God deal with your enemies.

How has God worked in your life?
He's not finished with you yet.

The mob, forty in number, gathered to plot to kill Paul. His nephew heard of an ambush and told Paul. (Acts 22:16) This let the commander of 1,000 troops to know this plan and order troops to protect Paul. He was saved because his nephew was in the right place. His nephew and the commander agreed and were used of the Lord to save Paul's life. Notice God had already told Paul to take courage because after he testified to his cause in Jerusalem, he would witness in Rome. (Acts 22:11) How has God worked in your life? Thank Him. He's not finished with you yet.

What has God called you to do? He will fulfill His purpose for you. The devil cannot touch you, and can only growl. (I John 5:18, 1 Peter 5:8) You must confess what you already possess! Paul already possessed life, at least until he got to Rome. (Acts 22:11) He chose to confess life and protection *in spite* of the circumstances. I am not moved by what I see or feel, but by what I believe. I believe the Word of God. Find out what you possess in God's Word and let it change your life and future as you confess it.

My Quiet Time Journal

1.   Ready yourself for a Fresh encounter with God. Pray and ask God to speak to you. (Psalm 37:7)

2.   Read the Scripture of the Day and prepare to hear a **Fresh Word** from God. (II Timothy 3:16-17)

3.   Respond with the ***"Mind of Christ"*** by writing down what God has said to you through the Scripture and the devotional thoughts. (Jeremiah 33:3)

4.   Reflect as you ***"Experience God"*** by listening to His Voice and writing down your prayers and thoughts. (John 16:23)

5.   Rely on Jesus to help you live out these truths. (Luke 11:28) Ask, ***"Lord, what do you want me to do today?"***   (God's to-do list.)

(Pray for strength as you put on the Full Armor of God.)

Acts 24:1-9

Citizens of Heaven, Citizens of Earth

Do you know any troublemakers? Do you remember any troublemakers in your school or neighborhood while growing up? Unfortunately, you may have some in your family. What is a troublemaker? According to Webster's dictionary, a troublemaker is one who incites others to quarrel, rebel, etc.

That was an accusation made against the Apostle Paul before Felix. He was accused of being a troublemaker. Was Paul really a troublemaker? Tertullus, a lawyer and professional orator for the Jews, said that Paul was troublemaker, stirring up riots among the Jews all over the world. (Acts 24:5) After reading chapters 21-23, we clearly see that this accusation was a false one. Wherever Paul went there was a R.I.O.T. (Righteous Invasion of Truth)!

You see, Paul had a passion for Jesus Christ. The Gospel overflowed from him everywhere he went. This caused a stir in the hearts of those seeking answers, and in those who thought they had all the answers.

Paul rebelled against the ways of darkness

Perhaps we could call Paul a righteous "troublemaker." Through his lifestyle and testimony of Jesus, as God gave him an open door, he urged people, in love, to rebel against the ways of darkness and to turn to Jesus, who is the Way, the Truth, and the Life. (John 14:6).

My Quiet Time Journal

1.   Ready yourself for a Fresh encounter with God. Pray and ask God to speak to you. (Psalm 37:7)

2.   Read the Scripture of the Day and prepare to hear a **Fresh Word** from God. (II Timothy 3:16-17)

3.   Respond with the *"Mind of Christ"* by writing down what God has said to you through the Scripture and the devotional thoughts. (Jeremiah 33:3)

4.   Reflect as you *"Experience God"* by listening to His Voice and writing down your prayers and thoughts. (John 16:23)

5.   Rely on Jesus to help you live out these truths. (Luke 11:28) Ask, *"Lord, what do you want me to do today?"*   (God's to-do list.)

(Pray for strength as you put on the Full Armor of God)

Acts 24:1-20

What Are You Striving For?

Paul was given the opportunity to defend himself regarding the accusations that were brought against him. He insisted that he was not the troublemaker that the Jews claimed he was. However, he admitted that he worshiped God, that he was a follower of The Way (or a follower of Jesus Christ), and that he believed everything that was in agreement with what was written in the Law and the Prophets. He even believed in the resurrection of the dead.

Paul said, "I strive always to keep my conscience clear before God and man." (Acts 24:16) In other words, Paul is saying, "I make this my constant business, to love God always, and to love my neighbor always." The word "strive" implies exercise, discipline, and something which is worked toward.

Paul worked at this every single day. Just like an athlete who goes through strict training to be the best, Paul exercised and disciplined himself spiritually to please God and win others to The Way. Paul sought to set the example of true discipleship and that included how to be a disciple. He knew he was responsible to train generation next.

Are you striving to please God or yourself?

Everything may not happen the way you plan, but "God causes all things to work for good to those who love Him, and who are called according to His purpose. (Romans 8:28) What are you striving for? Are you striving to please God or yourself? Strive to please God, and you'll be glad you did!

My Quiet Time Journal

1.   Ready yourself for a Fresh encounter with God. Pray and ask God to speak to you. (Psalm 37:7)

2.   Read the Scripture of the Day and prepare to hear a **Fresh Word** from God. (II Timothy 3:16-17)

3.   Respond with the *"Mind of Christ"* by writing down what God has said to you through the Scripture and the devotional thoughts. (Jeremiah 33:3)

4.   Reflect as you *"Experience God"* by listening to His Voice and writing down your prayers and thoughts. (John 16:23)

5.   Rely on Jesus to help you live out these truths. (Luke 11:28) Ask, *"Lord, what do you want me to do today?"*   (God's to-do list.)

(Pray for strength as you put on the Full Armor of God.)

Acts 24:23-27

No Compromise

In Acts 24:23, "Felix ordered the centurion to keep Paul under guard, but to give him some freedom and permit his friends to take care of his needs." A few days later Felix was with his wife, Drusilla, when he sent for Paul. Felix listened to Paul as he spoke about his faith in Christ (Acts 24:24). This would have been a perfect time for the Apostle to try to worm his way out of prison.

Instead of Paul trying to get out of prison through compromise, he spoke the Truth

This would have been a great time for Paul to compromise a little to get out of the mess that he was in. Surely he would back down from his stand on what he believed! I mean he could just water down the gospel a little bit to save himself and others. Did he do that? No! Instead, Paul began to speak about righteousness, self-control, and the judgment to come (Acts 24:25). You see, instead of Paul trying to get out of prison through compromise, he spoke the truth to Felix and Drusilla. He even confronted them concerning the sin in their lives. Felix was later afraid, told Paul to be quiet, and sent him away.

History tells us that Felix had taken Drusilla away from her first husband. Felix was a tyrant driven by sensual lust, and Paul knew that. Instead of having their curiosity satisfied, Felix and Drusilla were convicted of their sin. This landed Paul in prison for two years. "Felix was hoping that Paul would offer him a bribe" (Acts 24:26). Guess what? There was no compromise.

My Quiet Time Journal

1.   **Ready yourself** for a Fresh encounter with God. Pray and ask God to speak to you. (Psalm 37:7)

2.   **Read** the Scripture of the Day and prepare to hear a **Fresh Word** from God. (II Timothy 3:16-17)

3.   **Respond** with the *"Mind of Christ"* by writing down what God has said to you through the Scripture and the devotional thoughts. (Jeremiah 33:3)

4.   **Reflect** as you *"Experience God"* by listening to His Voice and writing down your prayers and thoughts. (John 16:23)

5.   **Rely** on Jesus to help you live out these truths. (Luke 11:28) Ask, *"Lord, what do you want me to do today?"*   (God's to-do list.)

(Pray for strength as you put on the Full Armor of God.)

Acts 25:1-12

God's Protection

There was a new governor in town named Festus. Three days after Fetus arrived, the Jewish leaders and chief priests wanted a favor from him. They hoped that he would transfer Paul from Caesarea to Jerusalem. Remember, more that forty Jews formed a conspiracy, and vowed that they would not eat until they killed the Apostle Paul.

Could you imagine someone being so angry with you that they would vow not to eat until you were injured or killed? Now, that is serious stuff!

Jesus had a plan for Paul

The Jews hoped that Festus would grant this favor. If he did, those Jews were prepared to set an ambush and kill Paul as he was taken into Jerusalem. But Jesus had a plan for Paul.

In Acts 23:11 the Lord Jesus stood near Paul and told him, "Take courage...you must testify in Rome." You see, it wasn't God's will for Paul to die on his way to Jerusalem. It was God's will for Paul to testify of Jesus in Rome. John 10:10 says the thief comes to kill, steal, and destroy. Satan was trying to kill Paul. He was trying to hinder the furtherance of the Gospel; however, it is hard to stop a person who is in the center of God's will. Paul was in the center of God's will, (although his circumstances made it appear otherwise). Always remember that if God has called you to do something, it will get done if you obey His way and seek to do His will.

The safest place in the world to be is in the will of God. Abide there!

My Quiet Time Journal

1.   Ready yourself for a Fresh encounter with God. Pray and ask God to speak to you. (Psalm 37:7)

2.   Read the Scripture of the Day and prepare to hear a **Fresh Word** from God. (II Timothy 3:16-17)

3.   Respond with the *"Mind of Christ"* by writing down what God has said to you through the Scripture and the devotional thoughts. (Jeremiah 33:3)

4.   Reflect as you *"Experience God"* by listening to His Voice and writing down your prayers and thoughts. (John 16:23)

5.   Rely on Jesus to help you live out these truths. (Luke 11:28) Ask, *"Lord, what do you want me to do today?"*   (God's to-do list.)

(Pray for strength as you put on the Full Armor of God.)

Acts 25:13-27

Jesus is Alive

Festus presented the case to King Agrippa and his sister Bernice. Festus brought in King Agrippa because he did not know how to handle the situation. Paul appealed to Caesar, and Festus agreed. Although Festus realized that the accusations brought against Paul by the Jews were not worthy of his death, he did not know what to write to Caesar concerning Paul's appeal. He did not want to waste his time. Knowing that King Agrippa understood Jewish affairs, Festus hoped that he would be able to make sense of the situation. This would allow Festus to have something to write as he sent Paul to Caesar.

As Festus explained the case to Agrippa and Bernice, we see an interesting contrast. Festus called Jesus a dead man, but Paul claimed that Jesus was alive.

Many in the world today believe that Jesus was a good man. Some say that He was a great prophet, but is now dead. But we Christians know that God raised Jesus from the dead, and that He is seated at the right hand of His Majesty on High. (Romans 8:34; Ephesians 1:20).

Can the world see the living Christ in you?

How can the world believe that Jesus is not some dead man, but is a Living Person? They can see Him through us, the Body of Christ! As the Father sent Jesus into the world to reveal Himself to man, so has He sent us!

Can the world see the living Christ in you? Are you loving your neighbor as Jesus commanded? He said that the world would know that we follow Him when we love one another (John 13:35). Let the living Christ live through you today!

Ask yourself, "How can I share His life with others today?"

My Quiet Time Journal

1.   Ready yourself for a Fresh encounter with God. Pray and ask God to speak to you. (Psalm 37:7)

2.   Read the Scripture of the Day and prepare to hear a **Fresh Word** from God. (II Timothy 3:16-17)

3.   Respond with the *"Mind of Christ"* by writing down what God has said to you through the Scripture and the devotional thoughts. (Jeremiah 33:3)

4.   Reflect as you *"Experience God"* by listening to His Voice and writing down your prayers and thoughts. (John 16:23)

5.   Rely on Jesus to help you live out these truths. (Luke 11:28) Ask, *"Lord, what do you want me to do today?"*   (God's to-do list.)

(Pray for strength as you put on the Full Armor of God.)

Acts 26:1-8

In Him We Have Hope

King Agrippa gave Paul an opportunity to defend himself Paul knew that Agrippa was well acquainted with all of the Jewish customs and controversies, so he asked Agrippa to really listen to him. Paul told him that he was on trial because of the hope that he had in God. What is hope? Hope is expectancy. A person that hopes is a person that expects something to happen in the future.

What was the hope that Paul had in God? It was the resurrection from the dead. You see, Paul was looking forward to and was expecting the resurrection from the dead. In 1 Thessalonians 4:16-18, Paul gives the church in Thessalonica a word of encouragement and a word of hope. It tells them that Jesus is coming again one day to gather to himself the saints who died in ages past and those who are alive at His coming. Paul says that there will be a resurrection one day and we will be with Jesus forever.

We as Christians can share in this hope that Paul described. To know that we will spend eternity with Jesus is an awesome fact!

There are many around us who do not have this hope. They are living lives of hopelessness. They think that there is nothing to live for and nothing to look forward to.

Give someone hope today! Remember, for Christians this earth is the only hell they will ever know. But for the sinner, who doesn't accept Christ as their Savior, this earth is the only heaven they will ever know! Think about that!

My Quiet Time Journal

1. **Ready yourself** for a Fresh encounter with God. Pray and ask God to speak to you. (Psalm 37:7)

2. **Read** the Scripture of the Day and prepare to hear a **Fresh Word** from God. (II Timothy 3:16-17)

3. **Respond** with the *"Mind of Christ"* by writing down what God has said to you through the Scripture and the devotional thoughts. (Jeremiah 33:3)

4. **Reflect** as you *"Experience God"* by listening to His Voice and writing down your prayers and thoughts. (John 16:23)

5. **Rely** on Jesus to help you live out these truths. (Luke 11:28) Ask, *"Lord, what do you want me to do today?"* (God's to-do list.)

(Pray for strength as you put on the Full Armor of God.)

Acts 26:9-32

A Divine Interruption

Paul explained to King Agrippa how he had once opposed the name of Jesus. Paul said that he had authority from the chief priests to have the Christians arrested and thrown into prison. Once the Christians were put to death, Paul would voice his approval. Then, things changed drastically for Paul. As Paul, then Saul, was on his way to Damascus to arrest more Christians, the Lord Jesus interrupted his journey! Jesus told Paul that he was chosen to go to the Gentiles (non-Jews), to open their eyes, so they could turn from Satan to God. God wanted their sins forgiven so that they would receive the inheritance that is in Christ.

God interrupts your life for a purpose.

Paul says to King Agrippa, "I was not disobedient to the vision from heaven: (Acts 26:19). You see, that is why Paul is in this situation. He was obeying what Jesus told him to do. How about you? Since Jesus came and divinely interrupted your life and saved you, have you been obedient to what He has commissioned you to do? (Matthew 28:19). Or have you been disobedient?

God has interrupted your life for a purpose: to save you from eternal damnation, and to help point others to Jesus, that their eyes may be opened and their sins forgiven. You are His disciple being prepared for service.

After Paul makes his appeal, Agrippa, Bernice and Festus realize that Paul was not doing anything worthy of death. Just as the Lord told him, Paul now sets out for Rome.

My Quiet Time Journal

1.   Ready yourself for a Fresh encounter with God. Pray and ask God to speak to you. (Psalm 37:7)

2.   Read the Scripture of the Day and prepare to hear a **Fresh Word** from God. (II Timothy 3:16-17)

3.   Respond with the **"Mind of Christ"** by writing down what God has said to you through the Scripture and the devotional thoughts. (Jeremiah 33:3)

4.   Reflect as you **"Experience God"** by listening to His Voice and writing down your prayers and thoughts. (John 16:23)

5.   Rely on Jesus to help you live out these truths. (Luke 11:28) Ask, **"Lord, what do you want me to do today?"**   (God's to-do list.)

(Pray for strength as you put on the Full Armor of God.)

Week Fourteen- Day One

Acts 27:1-13

God's Man

Paul's time had come to sail for Rome to appeal his case to Caesar. God showed favor on him by placing him under the centurion Julius, who treated Paul with kindness. (Acts 27:3).

Isn't it comforting to know that in the midst of trials and potentially dangerous situations, God lightens our load by placing "angels" in our midst? How many of us miss those lights in our world or forget to praise God for them because we're so focused on the darkness of our circumstances? Can we learn to look up and praise when the natural tendency is to look down and complain?

After days of difficult travel, Paul sensed danger and warned his companions in Acts 27:10-11:

"Men, I perceive that the voyage will certainly be attended with damage and great loss, not only of the cargo and the ship, but also of our lives. But the centurion was more persuaded by the pilot and the captain of the ship, than by what was being said by Paul."

Was Paul God's man? We would respond with a resounding "Yes!" Did the people listen to God's man? No! Turning instead to logic and worldly authority and to a majority vote (of worldly people) the decision was reached to sail on. (Acts 27:11-12).

Oh, Church of today! May we listen to God's man! When we see God's hand on a servant and repeatedly see God at work through him, let us not rely on what seems sensible or customary or even the people's voice. Let us listen to God Almighty who works in anything but traditional ways!

My Quiet Time Journal

1. **Ready yourself** for a Fresh encounter with God. Pray and ask God to speak to you. (Psalm 37:7)

2. **Read** the Scripture of the Day and prepare to hear a **Fresh Word** from God. (II Timothy 3:16-17)

3. **Respond** with the *"Mind of Christ"* by writing down what God has said to you through the Scripture and the devotional thoughts. (Jeremiah 33:3)

4. **Reflect** as you *"Experience God"* by listening to His Voice and writing down your prayers and thoughts. (John 16:23)

5. **Rely** on Jesus to help you live out these truths. (Luke 11:28) Ask, *"Lord, what do you want me to do today?"*   (God's to-do list.)

(Pray for strength as you put on the Full Armor of God.)

Acts 27:14-26

Who Is In Control?

Storms come, winds toss us about, and We lose control. (Acts 27:16). Like Paul, we find ourselves in a hurricane of life's circumstances. The worst of it seems to be that we can do nothing about it. We're no longer in charge. Someone or something has our life in turmoil. Whether it is relationships, illness, finances, persecution...whatever modern-day form it takes, the hurricane is almost certain to come and threaten to do us in. So the questions (doubts) start. "Does God really have a plan for my life?" "Why would He allow such a disaster in a Christian's life?" "Why do bad things happen to good people?" And so on and so on and so on.

STOP! Who made you? (Psalm 129:14). Who spoke the world into being? (Genesis 1:1). Who heals? (Luke 18:42). Who died on the cross, was buried, and walked in resurrection glory on this earth again? (Luke 24). Who changed your heart's desire from worldly endeavors to Spirit-led living when He saved you? (2 Corinthians 5:17). God, our Father. Has He changed? (Hebrews 13:8). Has He left Heaven and gone on vacation, leaving you to fend for yourself? (Hebrews 13:5). Has His power diminished with time? (Ephesians 1:18-23). Is His Word less true today than in former times? (1 Peter 1:25) NO! Read these scriptures again and be convinced.

Recently, when a family member became critically ill overnight, I was thrust into a hurricane. I faced the possibility of life alone. I was not in control. But just as God encouraged Paul through an angel telling him that all would be saved (Acts 27:24). God sent a fellow church member to be my messenger, my angel, to encourage and assure me. As the hurricane continued, I was encircled with God's Love. The storm didn't stop. Circumstances continued to rage, but God was and is constant. He wrapped His arms completely around me in an "inner-tub fashion.: I felt safe like when I was first shown how to float in an inner-tube. The Holy Spirit's constant Power and Presence daily filled my tube. I experienced firsthand that "peace that passes all understanding. (Phil. 4:7).

Paul, hearing from God through an angel, was encouraged. We will all be like Paul in a storm someday and in need of God's assurance. But we can also be that angel of encouragement to others who are in the midst of a storm. In whichever place we find ourselves, we can be content. God is in control

My Quiet Time Journal

1. **Ready yourself** for a Fresh encounter with God. Pray and ask God to speak to you. (Psalm 37:7)

2. **Read** the Scripture of the Day and prepare to hear a **Fresh Word** from God. (II Timothy 3:16-17)

3. **Respond** with the *"Mind of Christ"* by writing down what God has said to you through the Scripture and the devotional thoughts. (Jeremiah 33:3)

4. **Reflect** as you *"Experience God"* by listening to His Voice and writing down your prayers and thoughts. (John 16:23)

5. **Rely** on Jesus to help you live out these truths. (Luke 11:28) Ask, *"Lord, what do you want me to do today?"*   (God's to-do list.)

(Pray for strength as you put on the Full Armor of God.)

The Encourager

What does it take to be an encourager? In Paul's journey across the treacherous sea we have a prime example.

Paul uses good common sense in encouraging the men aboard the ship to eat. They had been without food for two weeks because they were watching the storm. God designed our bodies to respond to food and rest when we are stressed. Some sailors had even tried to make it on their own by using the life boat to get to shore. Paul made it know that all were in this together (Acts 27:34), and the men were made to remain on board. The life boat was cut loose and floated away. No more cheating. No more looking out for self. Paul showed us to follow God's design (care for the body) and follow God's word (spoken to Paul through the angel.) Paul was discipling generation next.

But what else did Paul do to encourage his companions? He hallowed God's name. In Acts 22:35 we see Paul in front of the total group giving thanks to God. Do we do this? Or do we allow Satan to fool us into thinking that it's okay to acknowledge God privately, but that public acknowledgement would be too embarrassing and might make some uncomfortable?

Did God plant a seed in one man's heart who watched Paul give thanks to his God? Did that man continue to listen to Paul witness for the remainder of the trip? Did one man accept Christ because of Paul's simple act of obedience and praise? Is what we say and do worth one man's soul? We are called to disciple.

God is the author of encouragement. God is the designer of the master plan. God is the one who will get us safely to shore – if we will follow and obey. We must commit to discipleship.

My Quiet Time Journal

1. **Ready yourself** for a Fresh encounter with God. Pray and ask God to speak to you. (Psalm 37:7)

2. **Read** the Scripture of the Day and prepare to hear a **Fresh Word** from God. (II Timothy 3:16-17)

3. **Respond** with the *"Mind of Christ"* by writing down what God has said to you through the Scripture and the devotional thoughts. (Jeremiah 33:3)

4. **Reflect** as you *"Experience God"* by listening to His Voice and writing down your prayers and thoughts. (John 16:23)

5. **Rely** on Jesus to help you live out these truths. (Luke 11:28) Ask, *"Lord, what do you want me to do today?"* (God's to-do list.)

(Pray for strength as you put on the Full Armor of God.)

Week Fourteen - Day Four

Acts 28:1-6

Contrast and Conclusions

At last, the storm was over. A warm welcome awaited Paul and the others as they arrived at Malta. The weather was cold and rainy, but a warm bonfire and hospitality were a welcome contrast to the trials of the last few weeks.

We can praise God in the midst of storms

Have you ever noticed how especially beautiful the sky looks after a storm? The clouds part and the sun seems to shine brighter than it ever has before. Or possibly a glorious rainbow appears. That is the way it is after the storms of life. Everyday things we once took for granted take on a new beauty. Life itself is invigorating. The contrast between the storm and the sun is what we notice. That is why when the storms come, we can praise God in the midst of them. Because we know the best is yet to come!

As Paul added wood to the warming fire, a snake bit his hand. (Acts 28:3). (Yes, bad things do happen to good people!) The natives expected Paul to drop dead, or at least to swell. But nothing happened. The people speculated in confusion. Was Paul a murderer or a god? (Acts 28:4-6)

How many of us do the same thing? We jump to conclusions at first glance without spending time finding out about a situation. And what's worse, many of us share our unsubstantiated opinions with others, never giving a thought to the harm that we might be doing in the process. Speculation, surface judging, - it's dangerous!

My Quiet Time Journal

1. **Ready yourself** for a Fresh encounter with God. Pray and ask God to speak to you. (Psalm 37:7)

2. **Read** the Scripture of the Day and prepare to hear a **Fresh Word** from God. (II Timothy 3:16-17)

3. **Respond** with the *"Mind of Christ"* by writing down what God has said to you through the Scripture and the devotional thoughts. (Jeremiah 33:3)

4. **Reflect** as you *"Experience God"* by listening to His Voice and writing down your prayers and thoughts. (John 16:23)

5. **Rely** on Jesus to help you live out these truths. (Luke 11:28) Ask, *"Lord, what do you want me to do today?"*   (God's to-do list.)

(Pray for strength as you put on the Full Armor of God.)

Week Fourteen - Day Five

Acts 28:7-10

Positive Chain

The sun continues to shine on Paul and his companions. Publius entertains the group at his estate for several days. How good God is to plan for such fine treatment of his people. Since Pubius father is ill, Paul ministers to him. He's not so involved with self and the pampering he's receiving that he doesn't respond to the man in need. He's not taking his well-deserved rest and time to recuperate alone, apart from the cares of the world. He lays hands on and prays for Publius father. (Acts 27:7-8). A true servant is always aware of ministry opportunities!

Do we practice random acts of kindness?

Hospitality must be important to God. Paul taught the Romans to "Share with God's people who are in need. Practice hospitality." (Romans 12:13). What is the usual response to kindness, to hospitality? Are we good to people who are good to us? Do we practice random acts of kindness? Do we return favors? More importantly, do we practice kindness to our own family members? Do we treat our children with respect? Do we put forth the effort with our spouse like we did when we were dating them? Or do we complain when we don't feel loved and appreciated at home? Did we disciple genuinely.

We need to develop positive chains. A kind word, a compliment, a shared duty, a warm response, an unselfish act, a generous sacrifice – all based in love – will link us together until we are encircled with that very love we gave away.

My Quiet Time Journal

1. **Ready yourself** for a Fresh encounter with God. Pray and ask God to speak to you. (Psalm 37:7)

2. **Read** the Scripture of the Day and prepare to hear a **Fresh Word** from God. (II Timothy 3:16-17)

3. **Respond** with the *"Mind of Christ"* by writing down what God has said to you through the Scripture and the devotional thoughts. (Jeremiah 33:3)

4. **Reflect** as you *"Experience God"* by listening to His Voice and writing down your prayers and thoughts. (John 16:23)

5. **Rely** on Jesus to help you live out these truths. (Luke 11:28) Ask, *"Lord, what do you want me to do today?"* (God's to-do list.)

(Pray for strength as you put on the Full Armor of God.)

Week Fourteen - Day Six

Acts 28:11-22

A, B, C, D, E

Upon arrival in Rome, Paul and those traveling with him were met by brothers who had heard they were coming. They made the effort to come from far away. This act of kindness encouraged Paul. He thanked God. Paul was allowed to live alone with only a soldier guarding him. (Acts 28:16).

He explained his position to his people, relating the circumstances of his arrest and near acquittal. But because the Jews had objected to his release, he was compelled to appeal to Caesar. His brothers were glad to hear his explanation, because even they had heard many stories about the situation. It was the topic of conversation everywhere.

Paul's Jewish brothers, though strangers to him, felt a real kinship to Paul – they were family – they had a common bond. So it is with the family of God. Because of our common experience with Christ (salvation) and our common motivation (the Holy Spirit within to guide and direct us) we, the Church, are a family. God has created us to be a part of a group, hold each other accountable, to have a sense of belonging, and to care for each other. We see here the beginning (or the ABC's) of Tender Loving Care groups.

Am I doing my part for the body of Christ?

How did the word of Paul's arrest spread so far away? Does the Gospel message have power? Does God intend for it to spread across the waters? To any student of the Bible, the answer is obvious. We are to disciple each other and evangelize our world for Christ. (Matthew 28:19). We must ask ourselves daily, am I doing my part in God's plan for the body of Christ?

My Quiet Time Journal

1. **Ready yourself** for a Fresh encounter with God. Pray and ask God to speak to you. (Psalm 37:7)

2. **Read** the Scripture of the Day and prepare to hear a **Fresh Word** from God. (II Timothy 3:16-17)

3. **Respond** with the **"Mind of Christ"** by writing down what God has said to you through the Scripture and the devotional thoughts. (Jeremiah 33:3)

4. **Reflect** as you **"Experience God"** by listening to His Voice and writing down your prayers and thoughts. (John 16:23)

5. **Rely** on Jesus to help you live out these truths. (Luke 11:28) Ask, **"Lord, what do you want me to do today?"** (God's to-do list.)

(Pray for strength as you put on the Full Armor of God.)

Acts 28:23-31

Proclaim the Kingdom of God

The Jewish leaders in Rome asked to meet with Paul. "They arranged to meet Paul on a certain day, and came in even larger numbers to the place where he was staying. From morning till evening he explained and declared to them the kingdom of God. He tried to convince them about Jesus from the Law of Moses and from the Prophets. Some were convinced by what he said, but others would not believe."(Acts 28:23-24). Again we see the model for the modern-day church. Scripture again reveals a pattern for us to follow in our journey with the Lord. We are to meet with God's man on a certain day in large numbers and listen to the open Word. We are told, pleaded with, and persuaded to put our faith in Christ.

Why do we have church? Why do we do this Sunday thing? Because God tells us to. (Exodus 2:8; Hebrews 10:25a). Because we have a model to follow, from Scripture. Because God placed within us a hunger and a desire to know Christ, who gives us new life, sustains us in the storm, directs us if we will listen, and leads us safely to shore. (John 12:32). But what about our friends and family members who won't listen? Those who won't believe, who do not agree with each other, and who leave? (Acts 28:24-25). God has said it will be so. "For the heart of this people has become dull, and with their ears they scarcely hear, and they have closed their eyes; lest they should see with their eyes, and hear with their ears, and understand with their heart and return, and I should heal them." (Acts 28:27).

The Gospel will continue to be presented. Even the ones we see as inferior are eligible to receive. (Acts 28:28). And many will listen! God knows who will and who won't respond. And God's faithful will continue to present the message of Truth! Will you, with your very life, proclaim the kingdom of God? Will you be a disciple maker?

Will you be like Pau and continue "unhindered preaching and teaching" about the Lord Jesus Christ? (Acts 28:31). Will you be an encourager? Will you listen when God speaks to you? Will you obey when your hear? Will you, with your very life, proclaim the Kingdom of God? Will you help us reach "Generation Next"?

My Quiet Time Journal

1. **Ready yourself** for a Fresh encounter with God. Pray and ask God to speak to you. (Psalm 37:7)

2. **Read** the Scripture of the Day and prepare to hear a **Fresh Word** from God. (II Timothy 3:16-17)

3. **Respond** with the *"Mind of Christ"* by writing down what God has said to you through the Scripture and the devotional thoughts. (Jeremiah 33:3)

4. **Reflect** as you *"Experience God"* by listening to His Voice and writing down your prayers and thoughts. (John 16:23)

5. **Rely** on Jesus to help you live out these truths. (Luke 11:28) Ask, *"Lord, what do you want me to do today?"* (God's to-do list.)

(Pray for strength as you put on the Full Armor of God.)

About the Author:

Dr. Garry Baldwin has ministered and Pastored Churches across North Carolina and has led Mission Teams around the World for over 40 years. Since 2004, he has served in Charlotte, North Carolina at Midwood Baptist Church in the Plaza Midwood/NoDa area. His love for discipleship inspired him to begin teaching at Charlotte Christian College and Theological Seminary to train and mentor Urban Pastors. A Graduate of The Citadel, Southeastern Baptist Theological Seminary, and Carolina Graduate School of Divinity, Dr. Baldwin seeks to challenge the Church to share the Gospel in their everyday life in a simple and clear way.

Dr. Baldwin has been married to Cheryl since 1976 and has 3 grown children and 2 grandchildren.

Made in the USA
Columbia, SC
24 November 2018